the office

THE OFFICIAL
PARTY PLANNING GUIDE
TO PLANNING PARTIES

DUNDER MIFFLIN, INC.
PAPER COMPANY

1725 SLOUGH AVENUE
SCRANTON, PA 18505

Party Planning Committee

the office

THE OFFICIAL
PARTY PLANNING GUIDE
TO PLANNING PARTIES

Authentic Parties, Recipes, and Pranks From
The Dundies to Kevin's Famous Chili

Written by Marc Sumerak

Recipes by Julie Tremaine

Crafts by Anne Taylor Murlowski

INSIGHT
EDITIONS

SAN RAFAEL · LOS ANGELES · LONDON

Art by Pam Beesly

TABLE OF CONTENTS

Introduction

Hello! It is my pleasure to inform you that by buying this book you have taken the first step toward creating your office's most esteemed unofficial organization: the Party Planning Committee. Be warned that this is not an undertaking for the faint of heart. One must have the perfect combination of drive, vision, and availability on Monday afternoons.

On the beloved TV series *The Office*, the Party Planning Committee is a group of employees dedicated to bringing every staff celebration to life in an unforgettable fashion. And with all of the holidays, birthdays, corporate events, and other random occasions that Michael Scott demanded they throw a party for, being an active part of the committee felt almost like having another full-time job. As on the show, this new position will likely not come with any additional pay—Wait! Come back! I wasn't finished!—but I can guarantee the look of moderate satisfaction on your colleagues' faces as they enjoy the fruits of your labor will certainly be reward enough.

The parties on *The Office* served many different purposes for different people. For Michael, they were the perfect opportunity to try out his latest batch of one-liners on a captive audience. But for the rest of the staff, they offered validation of a job well done, gave coworkers a chance to bond on a more personal level, and provided a temporary escape to the crushing boredom of the workday. Living up to that standard in your office sounds like a lot of pressure, but fortunately if you follow the advice of this book, you won't be alone.

While Angela and Phyllis jostled for the helm of the committee on the show, in reality the success of this committee depends on the participation of every member willing to put in the work. Even the Dwight of your office. With that in mind, enclosed please find a manual of advice gathered from some of Dunder Mifflin's PPCMVPPs (Party Planning Committee's Most Valuable Party Planners). I've also included a wide assortment of recipes, decorations, and games inspired by the show that are guaranteed to make your next gathering as festive as can be, no matter the occasion. Whether you're rolling out the red carpet for your annual company awards night or taking the team off-site for a well-deserved day at the beach, this guide has all the tips you need to become the next James Trickington.

Of course, even with this collection of inspirational ideas in hand, party planning is no easy task. On the show, the PPC was expected to pull off holiday miracles with virtually no time to prepare, no support from coworkers, and no budget for supplies. And while their committee chairs prepared to battle to the death over their differing visions for menus and décor, they always seemed to find something everyone could love. Or at least tolerate. Follow that example.

Despite the challenges, it's your job as a member of your new Party Planning Committee to stay focused on what is really important: that you are more than a group of people who work together. As Michael liked to say, the people you work with are, when you get down to it, your very best friends. And that's worth celebrating every day of the year. But since your budget likely only covers major milestones, that will have to do. Once the ice-cream cake has melted, though, you'll still have the memories. So make them count, and start planning now, because these parties won't throw themselves!

MICHAEL SCOTT'S SEXY/COOL/IMPORTANT PARTY

- Beer
- Light beer
- Streamers
- Orchids
- Better lighting
- Something made of ice
- Pizza with mushrooms
- Pizza without mushrooms
- White pizza
- Steak
- Chocolates
- Someone famous
- Cool music
- Confetti
- Go-go dancers

FUN TIP:

Spread the joy at work! Let's be honest: Sitting behind a desk for eight hours a day selling paper isn't most people's idea of fun. So when you find the chance to make a coworker's world a little brighter, take it. Corporate functions and birthdays are great to look forward to, but the days between official events can be long. Planning special bonus gatherings and activities can help everyone get through the daily grind. Whether you're dreaming up games for an impromptu Office Olympics or sharing the Finer Things as part of a secret club, the skills you acquire as a member of this committee can be applied to far more than just mandatory holiday parties. Be sure to use your new power wisely . . . and generously.

ONLINE RESOURCES:

Many of the signs, printed ephemera, and templates in this guide are available for you to download. You can either print out the templates or download the file to use with your favorite vinyl cutting machine. All templates are available for download on the online resources page at https://insighteditions.com/officeparties. Please refer to this URL whenever you see this symbol ⬇ in the book.

PARTY PLANNING COMMITTEE

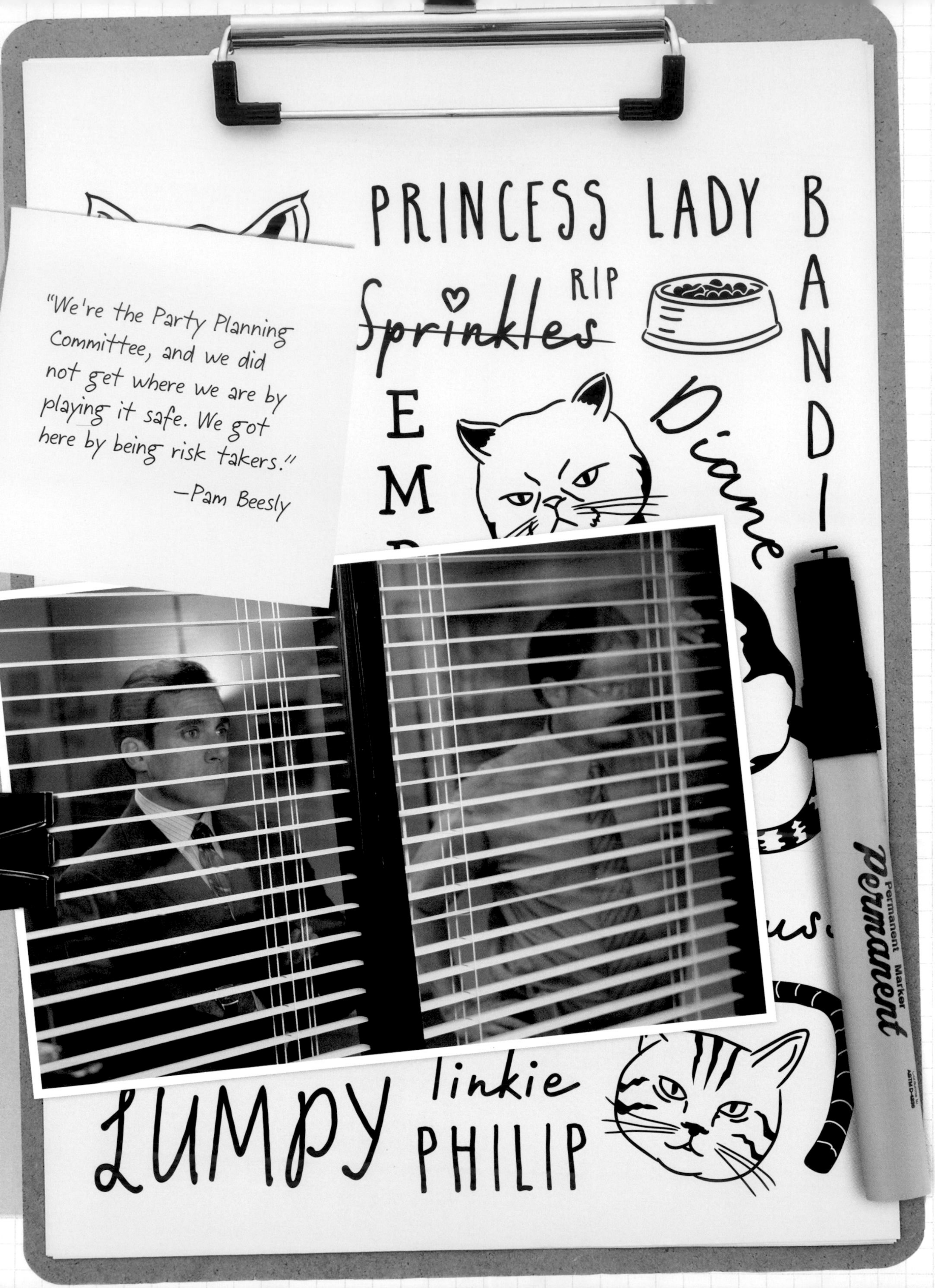
PRINCESS LADY
BANDIT
RIP
Sprinkles
Diane
LUMPY
Tinkie
PHILIP
Permanent Marker
Permanent

"We're the Party Planning Committee, and we did not get where we are by playing it safe. We got here by being risk takers."

—Pam Beesly

Party Planning Basics

> "Plan a party, Angela. Oh, and the entire world will see it. Oh! And here's $65 for your budget. Oh, and here are four idiots who'll do nothing but weigh you down. Oh, and your cat's still dead."
>
> —Angela Martin

Planning a party doesn't have to be an overwhelming experience. Here are a few tricks to make sure your next gathering goes off smoothly . . . or at least as smoothly as the parties at Dunder Mifflin usually go, which, now that I think about it, are rarely smooth.

Set a Budget

First things first: Set a budget. If you have a boss like Michael, he or she will most likely make big demands that push a party way over what you can actually afford. Instead, it's up to you to figure out your actual allotted expenditures in advance so that you can determine how many people can be invited, how much food needs to be purchased, and how many decorations and activities you're able to include.

If you are on a tight budget, limit the menu to snacks and iced tea with a starting time that falls between meals, so your partygoers aren't famished and expecting a four-course meal. Midafternoon parties are a great way to save on food costs! Booking a party from 2 p.m. to 4 p.m. means most folks will know to eat before or after. Unless one of your coworkers is a Kevin. (And even if he does eat before, he'll probably eat again at the party.)

Save receipts and keep track of everything you spend in a spreadsheet. This will help keep your budget on track and make sure you don't overspend. Because if your accounting department is anything like the Scranton branch's, you can bet: They. Are. Always. Watching.

Respect Each Other's Ideas

The Scranton Branch Party Planning Committee has had many members over the years, all with their own strong opinions about how to throw the perfect party. Some are old pros at planning company gatherings, like Angela, Phyllis, and Pam. Others, like Jim, Dwight, and Karen, just pitched in when needed (and then got out just as fast). With that many voices in the room, it was easy for some ideas to go unheard or for differences in party planning ideology to erupt into conflict.

As we saw on the show, forcing one's ideas into the mix without compromise results in parties where someone inevitably feels left out. It also creates unnecessary friction between committee members that can spill beyond the event itself. While you may be proud that you stuck to your guns, you still have to work with the person whose ideas you dismissed the next day. Work is stressful enough without adding extra tension because we couldn't agree over the color of streamers.

Even though the committee members didn't always see eye to eye, they knew it was almost impossible to do it all on their own. So if you happen to find yourself flying solo for some strange reason, trust me and nominate a few unofficial members to your own Party Planning Committee to help you spread out the responsibilities. Even help from the Kevin or the Creed of your office is better than no help at all.

Reserve a Venue

You'll want to determine where the party will happen early on in the planning process. A designated party space is ideal for helping keep everyone at the party close together, while providing a shared space for setting up food and drinks. No one wants to eat cake alone at their desk. Unless they're a Stanley.

For events that happen within your office, let the size of the gathering and number of people dictate the space, whether it's the break room, the conference room, or the warehouse. Off-site parties can be a good opportunity to get everyone out of their comfort zones. Local restaurants often have party rooms you can request for large groups. A restaurant reservation may require a minimum food and beverage purchase based on the room size. Confirm these details at the time you make the reservation, and make sure you keep an eye on your budget as you discuss food and drink minimums.

One last thing: If any of your fellow staff members have been, let's say, theoretically, banned for life from a local restaurant you were considering booking for your event, there are still other options. Community centers and libraries often offer large party rooms for group gatherings as well. Every space has different rules, so be sure to be respectful in case they don't allow confetti, thumbtacks, or delicious margaritas.

DUND
MIFFL
PAPER COM
1725 SLOUGH
SCRANTON, PA

"The Party Planning Committee is all over it. They've been working 24/7 all day yesterday."

—Michael Scott

Tasks to Delegate:

- **Pre-event setup**
- **Food**
- **Decorations**
- **Activities**
- **Cleanup crew**

If you ask each person to handle one or two party tasks, it makes getting everything organized and accomplished that much easier!

Alternatively, if you want to plan all the big items, such as decorations and activities, yourself, ask your party-planning crew to handle the food and drinks. A potluck-style event can make preparing for the party easier on the event host.

Invite the Guests

The most important part of throwing a party is making sure everyone knows when to show up! For bigger events, we usually put up posters a few weeks in advance so that everyone has all the necessary details. For birthdays, just circulate an internal e-mail the morning of the celebration. If you want to take a page out of Michael's book, just stand up and yell, "Conference room, five minutes!"

But if you really want to add a bit of extra class to the occasion, you can send out formal invitations that detail the date and time of the party, the event's theme, and whether or not guests should expect food and drinks. Try to invite guests as soon as you have the date set so that everyone can mark it in their calendars. Four to six weeks out is ideal, but if you actually have everything planned that far in advance, you probably don't need this manual.

Birthday Party

> *"Okay. So far, our ideal party consists of beer, fights to the death, cupcakes, blood pudding, blood, touch football, mating, charades, and yes, horse hunting."*
>
> —Jim Halpert

Good news! Even though it might not seem like it on the surface, there's one thing you automatically have in common with every single one of your coworkers: a birthday! And as long as yours doesn't fall on a holiday or a weekend, you can count on your colleagues to gather in the conference room with balloons, streamers, and banners to celebrate another year of you. Unless they forgot.

Planning a birthday party can be trickier than you might imagine. After all, a birthday is more than just a valid excuse to eat cake at 2 p.m. on a Wednesday. It's a celebration of life and a measure of the time you've all spent together. So make sure the person of honor gets the spotlight they deserve—and make sure your boss doesn't steal it for him or herself.

Even though birthdays make up the majority of the parties you'll probably throw at your office, each one should be unique. Unlike established holidays that have their own traditional treats and decorations, each birthday party should be adapted to reflect the individual tastes of the coworker being celebrated. For instance, on *The Office*, the PPC knew Meredith preferred devil's food cake, while Creed craved a nice peach cobbler, and, for some reason, Andy enjoyed mushroom caps. And then there's the matter of picking a theme. There's always a theme. (Sorry, "Birthday" and "Frosting" don't count.)

If some of your teammates' birthdays occur back-to-back (or if you managed to miss a few along the way), it might seem as though the simplest idea would be to combine them all into a larger communal celebration. Rookie mistake! Every member of your team deserves their own special day devoted solely to them. (Even your HR person, no matter what your boss says.) So make note of your coworkers' favorite colors, how their name is spelled, and their exact birth moments to help show them that you're fully aware of exactly how important they are.

FUN TIP:

Make sure you don't miss anyone's big day! If you do drop the ball somehow, it's a mistake they might never let you forget, so always keep your eyes on the weeks ahead to avoid having to scramble at the last minute (or, much worse, after the fact).

It Is Your Birthday. Cake

Whether rectangular or whale-shaped, everyone on *The Office* liked ice-cream cake. Well, except for Meredith (another thing, make sure to keep track of everyone's food allergies). That being said, if the birthday person can't do gluten or dairy, they aren't the only one who is going to be eating cake. So as long as you have something for them that meets their dietary restrictions, you can still serve the rest of the team the dessert they really want.

NOTE: This slab cake is frosted in and served from the same pan you bake it in. It's the easiest birthday cake around! The only difficult part is making sure you spell the birthday person's name correctly. I know that seems obvious, but as we saw on the show, mistakes were made.

Prep Time: 15 minutes
Cook Time: 40 minutes
Yield: 12 servings

FOR THE CAKE:

3 cups all-purpose flour
3 cups granulated sugar
¾ cup best-quality cocoa powder
1 teaspoon salt
2 teaspoons baking soda
2 teaspoons baking powder
1½ teaspoons espresso powder
1¼ cups buttermilk
¾ cup vegetable oil
2 teaspoons pure vanilla extract
3 eggs
1 cup hot water
Nonstick cooking spray

FOR THE VANILLA BUTTERCREAM FROSTING:

½ cup (1 stick) salted butter, room temperature
2 egg whites
1 teaspoon pure vanilla extract
4 cups confectioners' sugar

Red food coloring (optional, for decoration)
Orange candy gum (for decoration)

"I guess my only wish would be that nothing so terrible would ever happen to anyone else ever again."

—Kelly Kapoor

1. Preheat the oven to 350°F.

2. Prepare the cake. In a medium mixing bowl, combine the flour, sugar, cocoa powder, salt, baking soda, baking powder, and espresso powder. Mix to combine, and set aside.

3. In the bowl of a stand mixer fitted with a flat beater, combine the buttermilk, vegetable oil, and vanilla extract on medium-low speed until incorporated, about 1 minute.

4. Add the dry mixture to the stand mixer in thirds, allowing 1 minute of mixing between each addition.

5. With the mixer running on medium speed, add the eggs one at a time, allowing 1 minute between each addition. Next, slowly add the hot water (make sure it is very hot) over the course of about 2 minutes.

6. Spray a 9-by-13-inch glass or ceramic baking pan with cooking spray. Pour batter into the pan, and bake for 35 to 40 minutes, until a toothpick inserted into the center of the cake comes out clean. Remove from the oven, and allow to cool.

7. While the cake is cooling, prepare the frosting. Combine the butter, eggs, and vanilla extract in the bowl of a stand mixer fitted with a flat beater. Beat on medium-low to combine, and then add the sugar in thirds, allowing 1 minute between additions. Increase speed to medium-high, and mix until the frosting is smooth and creamy.

8. If you'd like to create a cake fit for Kelly Kapoor, remove a quarter of the frosting to a separate bowl, and add a couple of drops of red food coloring. Mix to create pink frosting. Then, using either a piping bag fitted with a piping tip or a large plastic zip-top bag, place the bag into a large cup or pitcher. Fold down the edges of the bag around the exterior of the container, and then scoop the pink frosting into the bag. Remove the bag from the container, and seal the top. If using a plastic zip-top bag, cut a small hole at the bottom of the bag to create the tip. Gently but firmly squeeze the top of the bag so the frosting moves to the bottom of the bag and is ready to use.

9. Make sure the cake is cooled completely, and leaving it in the pan, frost the top of the cake with the white frosting, using a cake spatula or rubber spatula to create a smooth top. If using the pink frosting, write "HAPPY B'DAY" and the birthday person's name. Be sure to spell their name correctly! For the final flourish, place a single orange candy gum in the middle of the cake.

Alfredo's Pizza Café Pizza

With so many pizza joints out there, ordering delivery can be confusing. One simple mistake and you've spent $60 on hot circles of garbage that no one wants to eat. Now you can avoid the hassle (and a potential hostage situation) by making your own pizza.

Most offices don't have an oven on hand, but no matter where you end up baking this, it's guaranteed to please. You can even use a pizza stone to give your crust that classic crispy bottom. But if you don't have one, a standard baking sheet works just fine.

Prep Time: 45 minutes, including time to rise
Cook Time: 12 minutes
Yield: Two 12-inch pizzas

FOR THE PIZZA DOUGH:

1 packet instant yeast
1¾ cups warm water
4 tablespoons olive oil, divided
1 teaspoon kosher salt
½ teaspoon sugar
5 cups bread flour, plus more for dusting
¼ cup cornmeal

FOR THE PIZZAS:

1 cup tomato sauce, divided
2 balls fresh mozzarella, sliced
20 small basil leaves
Kosher salt and black pepper, to taste

1. In the bowl of a stand mixer fitted with a dough hook, place the yeast, water, 3 tablespoons olive oil, salt, and sugar. Mix on low for 30 seconds to combine. Then, while the mixer is running, gradually add the flour to the bowl. This should take at least 2 minutes.

2. Increase speed to medium, and mix for 6 to 8 minutes until a firm ball forms that pulls away from the sides of the bowl. If the dough is very sticky, add a few tablespoons of flour. If the dough is too dry, add a tablespoon of water.

TIP: If you don't have a stand mixer, you can easily mix this dough by hand by adding the dough ingredients into a bowl, mixing with a wooden spoon until the dough comes together. Lightly flour a work surface and turn the dough out and begin kneading until the dough is smooth and elastic, about 7 minutes.

3. Remove the dough from the mixer, and then cut in half. Coat both dough balls with the remaining olive oil, and then cover and allow to sit for at least 30 minutes, or up to 1 hour.

4. While the dough is resting, preheat the oven to 475°F with a pizza stone inside. The pizza stone should be heated to oven temperature before using, which will take at least 30 minutes. Once the pizza stone is hot, leave it in the oven, and don't try to remove it until it's cool.

5. On a lightly floured surface, roll out each ball into a 12-inch disc. You can do this with your hands, but you may need to stretch the dough as far as it can go, let it rest for 5 minutes, and then stretch it to its full size.

6. Dust a cutting board or pizza board with cornmeal, and then place the dough on top, and top with ½ cup tomato sauce, the slices from 1 ball of mozzarella, 10 basil leaves, and salt and pepper to taste. Carefully transfer the assembled pizza from the board onto the pizza stone in the oven. The easiest way to do this is to place the board next to the stone in the open oven, then slide across to the other surface. Repeat the process with the other dough and toppings. If you don't have a pizza stone, simply prepare the pizza on a baking sheet, then slide the sheet into the oven to bake.

7. Bake for 10 to 12 minutes, until the crust is golden brown. Remove from the oven by transferring back onto the cutting board—*not* by picking up the hot pizza stone. Cut into slices, and serve hot.

Mini "Big Tuna" Melts

Who needs an eight-foot party sub (or even eight one-foot subs) when you could have these bite-size beauties? Be forewarned: Although anyone would be proud to serve these sammies, be careful eating them around the Andy of your office or you might find yourself permanently branded "Little Tuna," "Big Tuna 2: The Sequel," "Hot Tunette," or something equally mortifying. Note: If some of your coworkers aren't fond of fishy finger foods, you can always go with a classic crowd-pleaser, like bologna, tomato, and ketchup, instead.

Prep Time: 10 minutes
Cook Time: 12 minutes
Yield: 15 servings

¼ cup mayonnaise
2 tablespoons Dijon mustard
¼ cup minced red onion
¼ cup minced banana peppers
1 stalk celery, minced
1 tablespoon dried parsley, or 2 tablespoons fresh
Two 6-ounce cans tuna in water, drained
1 baguette, cut into 15 ¼-inch-thick round slices
Olive oil spray, or olive oil
3 plum tomatoes, each cut into 5 round ¼-inch-thick slices (for a total of 15), seeds removed
4 slices American cheese, cut into quarters

> "Party planning is literally the stupidest thing I've ever done in my life."
> —Jim Halpert

1. Preheat the oven to 425°F.

2. In a medium bowl, combine the mayonnaise, mustard, red onion, banana peppers, celery, parsley, and tuna. Mix well, breaking up any large chunks.

3. Line a baking sheet with foil, and lay out the bread slices. Use the olive oil spray or use a pastry brush to add a light layer of olive oil on both sides of each baguette slice. Spoon a generous tablespoon of tuna onto each, then top with a slice of tomato and a piece of cheese.

4. Bake until the cheese is melted and golden brown, about 10 to 12 minutes. Serve.

TIP: If your office has a toaster oven, you can make these in the office doing a few batches at a time.

ADDITIONAL TIP: It's common courtesy to not cook fish in the break room, so make sure that you prep these somewhere else. Preferably somewhere far away. Like, maybe the microwave in the warehouse.

17

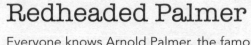

Redheaded Palmer

Everyone knows Arnold Palmer, the famous golfer who had an even-more-famous drink named after him. But not nearly enough people know Meredith Palmer, the Dunder Mifflin supplier relations rep who once drank so much at an office party that her hair caught on fire (while she continued dancing, blissfully unaware). A legend like that deserves a drink—a particularly boozy one—named after her, too! So here it is. Enjoy!

Prep Time: 5 minutes
Yield: 1 serving

3 ounces iced tea
1½ ounces lemonade
1½ ounces bourbon
Lemon wheel or blood orange slice, for garnish

1. Fill a highball glass with ice.

2. Add the liquids. Stir to combine.

3. Garnish with a lemon wheel, and serve.

"Good news. You're not actually a year older, because you work here, where time stands still."
—Stanley Hudson

CRAFTS

It Is Your Birthday. Banner

A birthday banner to recognize the guest of honor is an important way to make sure everyone knows the facts about what exactly your group is celebrating. If you're like Pam, with her artistic background, you'll likely want signage with thoughtful design elements that tie into the theme of the celebration. However, some of your coworkers may tend to be a bit more direct in their messaging. For instance, the banner Dwight and Jim created for Kelly certainly made a statement . . . but that's literally all it did. While the best way to print this banner is with an old-school dot matrix printer, you probably don't have one of those on hand. These instructions walk you through how to set up the file to print from your favorite word processing software. It's probably not the strongest choice, but if you are running out of time to plan, it is your banner.

SUPPLIES

- **8½-by-11-inch printer paper**
- **Computer**
- **Word processing software**
- **Printer**
- **Clear tape**

1. Open the word processing software on your computer.

2. Set the page height in your word processing software to 11 inches and the width to 54 inches.

3. Add a text box, and set the font to Arial and the size to 325.

4. Type "It is your birthday." Don't forget the period! It is a statement of fact.

5. If you're printing from home, the banner will print across several 8½-by-11-inch sheets of printer paper. Once printed, tape together and hang to complete your decor.

TIP: If you prefer a solid banner similar to the one Dwight created, save the file and head to your favorite print shop for printing.

Hockey Jerseys

All of your coworkers deserve an amazing birthday bash. Consider a Michael Scott party. It has to be next-level cool. And what could possibly be cooler than a trip to the local skating rink? Before you hit the ice, invite everyone at the party to create their own customized hockey jersey using their favorite—or least favorite—nicknames, from "Nard Dog" to "Boner Champ"! Be sure to purchase enough shirts for everyone in attendance at the party.

SUPPLIES

- **Computer**
- **Word processing software**
- **Printer**
- **Oversize 100% cotton long-sleeve shirts**
- **Cardboard**
- **Fabric paint**
- **Painter's tape**
- **Foam brushes**
- **Small paintbrushes**
- **Ruler**

HOCKEY JERSEY INSTRUCTIONS

1. Open the word processing software on your computer. Set your font to a bold font such as Impact and set the font size anywhere from 500 to 600. Type out the numbers 0 to 9, which will print over multiple pages to work as 8- to 9-inch-tall stencils. Cut out each of these numbers.

2. Cut a piece of cardboard approximately the same width as the shirt you plan to paint on. Slip this inside the shirt as it will help stabilize the shirt for painting and keep the paint from bleeding through.

3. Turn the jersey so the back is facing up. Place one of the number stencils so it is centered in the middle of the jersey. (Michael's jersey uses the number 1, so you should pick something else for yours.) Using the painter's tape, tape around the stencil, using it as a guide to create an outline of the number on the jersey. You can use multiple layers of tape to prevent the paint from seeping beneath the tape. Remove the stencil.

4. Using painter's tape, add a line from shoulder to shoulder that is approximately 2 inches below the neckline on the back of the shirt. Measure 3 inches below that, and add a second piece of tape. This is the area where you will put the name. We recommend using a pencil to sketch out the name before painting. Or, if you want to make sure your party attendees know who gave them their jerseys, you can instead write "From *your name*" on the back of the jersey, in honor of Dwight's gift to Michael.

TIP: When painting on the back of the shirt, start at the top by writing the name, and then move on to the number. This will allow you to keep your arm out of the paint while you work.

5. Pour a small amount of the fabric paint into a dish or cup. Using a small brush, paint the name you wish to display on the back of your shirt between the name lines placed in step 4. Letters should be the full height of the space and written in uppercase block letters.

6. Using a foam brush, add a thin layer of paint over the number area.

7. Leave the shirt to dry. This may take a few hours.

8. Once the back is fully dry, flip over and decorate the front with your favorite team's name or even the Dunder Mifflin logo!

DUNDER MIFFLIN, INC.
PAPER COMPANY

1725 SLOUGH AVENUE
SCRANTON, PA 18505

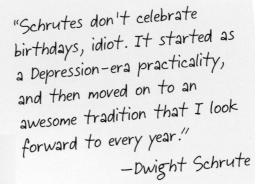

"Schrutes don't celebrate birthdays, idiot. It started as a Depression-era practicality, and then moved on to an awesome tradition that I look forward to every year."

—Dwight Schrute

World's Best Boss Coffee Mug or Dunder Mifflin Mug

When Michael was the boss he was many things, but World's Best? Ehh . . . Regardless, that never stopped him from flaunting this mug. Feel free to give this to your boss whether or not it's true, as apparently it doesn't really matter.

If you want, you can add your own personal touches to create a custom gift worthy of any birthday celebration. The designs can be hand drawn or placed using vinyl cut stencils. Just download the World's Best Boss Mug and Dunder Mifflin Mug templates from the online resources page.

SUPPLIES
- **White coffee mugs**
- **Vinyl cutter machine (optional)**
- **Adhesive vinyl sheets (optional)**
- ⬇ **Dunder Mifflin Mug logo templates (optional)**
- **Pencil**
- **Black oil-based permanent marker or glass paint markers**
- **Oven**

1. Wash and dry the mugs thoroughly. This will ensure that the marker is able to properly affix to the glass.

2. If using a vinyl stencil, cut out the template using your vinyl cutter machine, and remove the letters from within the template to create the stencil. Then carefully remove the stencil and—making sure it's positioned exactly where you want it to be—apply to the surface of your mug. If you choose to freehand the design, use a pencil first to outline where you want to use the marker.

3. Carefully fill in the design with a black marker. This will take 2 to 5 minutes to dry. Once fully dry, remove the vinyl.

4. Place your mugs in a cool oven, and then set your oven to 350°F, or follow your pen's manufacturer's instructions. Allow the oven to come to temperature, and bake the mugs for 20 minutes to set the paint. Remove and allow to cool.

TIP: Your handmade mugs are not dishwasher safe. To preserve the design, hand wash only.

MICHAEL SCOTT
REGIONAL MANAGER

"Let's hope the only downsizing that happens to you is that someone downsizes your age."
—Michael Scott

FUNTIVITIES

Coffee Mug Basketball

Here's a great party activity that also happened to be Pam's favorite way to break up the day!

1. Each player is provided 3 paper clips and 3 small paper balls.

2. Set the mug on a table, and mark the ground away from the coffee mug at 2 feet, 4 feet, and 6 feet. These are your throw lines.

3. Players must stand at the first throw line and attempt to lob items into the mug one at a time. After successfully sinking a paper clip and paper ball, players may advance to the next throw line.

4. The player with the most items successfully tossed into the mug wins.

Hockey Uniform Relay

Feel free to use real uniform items if you have access to a complete hockey uniform. If you don't, assemble the following items for each team:

- **Oversize Hockey Jersey or shirt (page 20)**
- **2 throw pillows**
- **A baseball cap or bike helmet**
- **Tissue boxes (as skates)**

1. Divide into 2 teams of equal numbers. Mark the floor in two spaces 10 feet apart. This is where players must run once fully dressed.

2. Players must race to completely dress in the jersey with pillows on their shoulders, a baseball cap on backward, and 2 tissue-box skates on their feet.

3. Once fully clothed, they must run the length of the relay and return, where the next teammate will assist them in removing the "hockey uniform" before proceeding in the race. The team who has all players over the finish line first is the winner.

DÉCOR

Although an office conference room may not be the most appealing place to celebrate a birthday, you can jazz up the drab of any room using a few thoughtfully placed decorations, and make it a party everyone will be jealous of. Hang bright streamers and balloons in your officemate's favorite colors, and be sure to bring food such as your homemade version of Alfredo's Pizza Café Pizza (page 16) and the Redheaded Palmer (page 18).

If, for some reason, you want to emulate the less-than-spectacular birthday party Dwight and Jim put together for Kelly, try the below:

Hang the It Is Your Birthday. Banner (page 19) on the wall using large pieces of masking tape. Ideally, this should be near the food display or where everyone can see it upon entering the room.

Underinflate several brown, black, and silver balloons. No one wants bright colors at their party! Use several pieces of visible masking tape to hang streamers from the ceiling, and attach the balloons to the bottom of the streamers, letting them hang down roughly around or slightly above head level.

Any remaining streamers can be draped throughout the room and secured with masking tape.

Serve the It Is Your Birthday. Cake (page 14). Top the dessert with candles or numbers displaying your best guess at the birthday person of honor's age. Anything close will do.

If fun is deemed necessary, activities can be found on the opposite page, allowing you to prove your worth as you lead your coworkers in a round of team building exercises.

Alternately, if you are the rank of Assistant to the Regional Manager or higher, you may grant the birthday person a choice of either an hour of television or an hour of napping. But not one minute longer. It's a workday, people.

The Dundies

> *"You know what they say about a car wreck, where it's so awful you can't look away? The Dundies are like a car wreck that you want to look away, but you have to stare at it because your boss is making you."*
>
> —Pam Beesly

Every year, the Scranton branch of Dunder Mifflin holds an awards night called the Dundies. Michael said it was an evening dedicated to recognizing his team's individual accomplishments, but we all know that it was really an excuse for him to polish his stand-up routine in front of a group of people who could potentially be fired if they didn't laugh. Very little at the Dundies wasn't cringey, but thankfully there was an open bar to ease the pain.

Just because it was a nightmare for them, doesn't mean you can't make an office awards night fun. Your company probably has plenty of unsung heroes who deserve a night like this to give them a little extra attention. The Oscars, Kevins, and Darryls of your office have spent 9,986,000 minutes of their lives bringing out the best in what you do, so it's only fair that you take one evening a year to show them their contributions have been vaguely noted.

Sure, an awards ceremony might sound a little lavish, but don't worry: Black-tie attire is strictly optional. The Dundies weren't about being fancy. They were about celebrating the strengths—and, unfortunately, in some cases, the weaknesses—of the employees. So whether you're a "Promising Assistant Manager," the office's "Busiest Beaver" (make sure to double-check the spelling on that one!), or just have the "Whitest Sneakers," your Dundies can be a night to bring your co-workers all together by focusing on what sets you all apart.

Now, pump up the volume on your karaoke machine, because it's showtime!

FUN TIP:

Encourage your host to mix up the awards and praise . . . and at the very least convince them to not give an award like "Hottest in the Office," especially not to the same person for the sixth year in a row. Not only is it completely subjective, but it will likely lead to a mandatory meeting with HR.

Fajitas

If you've ever wanted to hear how good your food tastes, look no further than fajitas. But make these steaming-hot platters of grilled meats or veggies because they're delicious, not because you think their sizzle will drown out your host's witty repartee. They won't. Nothing ever does.

Prep Time: 90 minutes (including chill time)
Cook Time: 20 minutes
Yield: 4 servings

FOR FAJITA SEASONING:

2 teaspoons chili powder
1 teaspoon salt
1 teaspoon smoked paprika
1 teaspoon onion powder
1 teaspoon garlic powder
½ teaspoon cayenne pepper
½ teaspoon cumin

FOR PICO DE GALLO:

1 small white onion, minced
1 to 2 medium jalapeños, minced with seeds removed
Juice of 2 limes
½ cup fresh cilantro
1 teaspoon salt
1 pound firm, ripe tomatoes

FOR FAJITAS:

2 tablespoons neutral cooking oil
1½ pounds chicken breast, steak, or extra-firm tofu
1 green bell pepper, sliced into ¼-inch strips
1 yellow or red pepper, sliced into ¼-inch strips
1 large yellow onion, sliced into ¼-inch strips
Fajita seasoning (see recipe above)
12 flour tortillas
Pico de gallo (see recipe above)
Sour cream, guacamole, and shredded cheddar cheese, as garnish

"The Dundies are all about coming together! And recognizing the indomitability of the human spirit!"
—Deangelo Vickers

1. Prepare the fajita seasoning. Combine all ingredients in a small bowl. Adjust spices to taste, and set aside.

2. Prepare the pico de gallo. In a medium bowl, combine the onion, jalapeño, lime juice, cilantro, and salt. Let marinate while you dice the tomatoes. Make sure to discard the tomatoes' seeds and pulp, and to make the pieces as small as possible. Add the tomatoes to the mixture, and then refrigerate for at least 1 hour.

3. Prepare the fajitas. In a large cast-iron skillet, heat the cooking oil on medium-high. Add your protein, and cook for 5 minutes on one side, then flip and cook for an additional 5 minutes. Adjust as needed if meat is starting to burn. Remove to a plate to rest.

4. In the same pan, cook the vegetables until softened, about 5 minutes.

5. Slice the steak or chicken into thin strips against the grain, or slice the tofu into cubes if using.

6. Add the protein back into the pan, as well as the fajita seasoning and ⅓ cup of water. Cook until the water is absorbed and everything is heated through, about 3 minutes.

7. Warm the tortillas by wrapping the stack in a damp paper towel and then in aluminum foil. Bake in a 300°F oven for about 10 minutes, until warm.

8. Serve the fajitas and tortillas family-style, and let everyone assemble their own, using pico de gallo, sour cream, guacamole, and cheese as toppings.

Extra-Awesome Mini Onion Blossoms

What's more awesome than an onion? A lot of things, actually. But what's *extra* awesome is an onion cut into the shape of a flower blossom and deep-fried! To kick it up to maximum awesomeness, pair it with your favorite awesome sauce. We recommend a spicy curry. Did I mention these were awesome?

Prep Time: 20 minutes
Cook Time: 12 minutes
Yield: 20 pieces

FOR THE DIPPING SAUCE:

½ cup sour cream
¼ cup mayonnaise
1 tablespoon ketchup
½ teaspoon Worcestershire sauce
2 teaspoons grated horseradish
½ teaspoon smoked paprika
½ teaspoon garlic powder
½ teaspoon salt
Pinch of cayenne pepper, to taste

FOR THE BLOSSOMS:

20 cipollini onions
1 cup milk
2 eggs
½ cup fine breadcrumbs
½ cup all-purpose flour
1 teaspoon garlic powder
1 teaspoon onion powder
1 teaspoon salt
1 teaspoon dried parsley
1 teaspoon smoked paprika
½ teaspoon black pepper
½ teaspoon cayenne pepper
3 cups neutral cooking oil

1. Prepare the dipping sauce. Combine all ingredients in a small bowl, and stir to combine. Refrigerate at least 30 minutes to allow flavors to combine.

2. Prepare the blossoms. First, carefully cut off the root end of each onion so that just the roots are removed but most of the flesh remains intact. Peel the onion.

3. Lay the onion so the tip of the onion is facing down. Make three slices across the top so that the cuts intersect in the middle and there are six wedges of equal size. Do not cut all the way through the onion, and make sure you're leaving the tip of the onion intact to hold the onion together. Spread out the layers of onion as much as possible without breaking them off the main piece. Repeat for all onions.

4. In a medium bowl, whisk together the milk and eggs to create the wet mixture.

5. In another medium bowl, combine the breadcrumbs, flour, garlic powder, onion powder, salt, parsley, paprika, black pepper, and cayenne pepper. Stir to combine.

6. In a large, high-sided skillet or Dutch oven, heat the oil on medium-high heat until the temperature reaches 300°F, or the tip of a wooden utensil bubbles when touched to the surface.

7. While the oil is heating, batter the onions. Working in batches, dip a few onions into the dry mixture, then the wet mixture, then back into the dry mixture. Try to get as much breading as possible down into the layers.

8. Fry the onions in small batches until golden brown, taking care not to overcrowd the pan, about 3 to 4 minutes. Allow the oil to come back up to temperature between each batch. Serve with the dipping sauce.

Sizzling Queso Dip With Chorizo

These bubbling skillets of hot, gooey cheese and chorizo are the perfect side for your fajitas, though they can double as a great appe-teaser, too. Just be sure to make a few extra if you want to guarantee you'll get some before they disappear.

Prep Time: 10 minutes
Cook Time: 35 minutes
Yield: 6 servings as an appetizer

8 ounces chorizo, crumbled with casings removed
¼ cup minced yellow onion
2 cloves garlic, minced
¼ cup roasted green chiles
16 ounces Oaxaca cheese, freshly grated (or a soft cheese like Monterey Jack or mozzarella)

1. Preheat the oven to 400°F.

2. In a medium skillet, cook the chorizo over medium-high heat until the fat renders and the meat is browned and crispy, about 10 minutes. Remove to a paper towel-lined plate to drain.

3. In the same skillet, cook the onion and garlic over medium-high heat in the rendered chorizo fat until golden brown, about 5 minutes. Add the chorizo back into the pan, followed by the chiles, and stir to combine.

4. In an 8-by-10-inch baking dish, layer a third of the cheese along the bottom of the dish. Top evenly with slightly less than half of the meat mixture. Sprinkle another third of the cheese across the pan, followed by another layer of meat, but reserve a few tablespoons of the meat mixture. Finish with the last of the cheese, and then top with the last few tablespoons of the meat.

5. Bake until the cheese is browned and bubbling, about 20 minutes.

Second Drink Margaritas

Did corporate put the kibosh on covering the tab for an open bar this year? Don't fret quite yet! Just one of these mighty margaritas packs a solid punch all on its own . . . but after you think the glass is empty, you're in for a special surprise. The ice melts, and then it's like a second drink!

Prep Time: 5 minutes
Yield: 1 serving

2 round jalapeño slices, seeded
Juice of 1 lime
Juice of ½ an orange
1½ ounces mezcal
1½ ounces orange liqueur
Salt, for the rim

1. In a shaker, muddle the jalapeño with the lime and orange juices. Add the mezcal and orange liqueur, fill with ice, and shake until cold.

2. Use the lime you just juiced to moisten the rim of a rocks glass, and dip the glass in the salt. Fill the glass with ice.

3. Strain the cocktail into the glass, and serve.

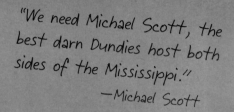

"We need Michael Scott, the best darn Dundies host both sides of the Mississippi."
—Michael Scott

"Was tonight a success? Well, I made Pam laugh so hard she fell down and almost broke her neck. So I killed, sort of."
—Michael Scott

DUNDIE AWARD
Bushiest Beaver Award

DUNDIE AWARD
Fine Work

DUNDIE AWARD
Whitest Sneakers

DUNDIE AWARD

CRAFTS

DIY Dundies

An awards night without awards is just another night. But in the eventuality that your local trophy shop is unable to stay afloat, here's an easy way to make custom homemade Dundies. All it will cost is a bit of extra time and a touch of creativity to make something that your colleagues will be proud to put in a display case above their bed (or keep hidden so they don't look at them and get cocky).

If you want, you can even make an extra one for yourself. Go ahead, you deserve it!

SUPPLIES

- ⬇ **Briefcase Template**
- **Repurposed, thrifted, or discount store sports trophies featuring a person**
- **Computer**
- **Color printer**
- **Glue stick**
- **Hot-glue gun**
- **Yellow or gold poster board**
- **Black pen**

1. Print out the briefcase template from the online resources. If possible, use a heavier paper than standard printer paper. Fold the briefcase along the dotted line, and then use the glue stick to glue the briefcase together.

2. Once dry, use a hot-glue gun to attach the briefcase to the hand of the figure on the trophy.

3. Then, cut a piece of poster board so it is the same size as the trophy's name plate. Write the award title on it with a black pen, and affix over the trophy's nameplate with the hot-glue gun.

TIP: If you want to keep your coworkers engaged in the Dundies, make a game out of predicting this year's winners before the host announces them. As guests arrive, have them write their guesses on a piece of paper and place them in an empty margarita glass. After the show, read the submitted guesses to the group and see how close you got!

THE DUNDIES

- **Busiest Beaver**
- **Hottest in the Office**
- **Tight-Ass**
- **Spicy Curry**
- **Don't Go in There After Me**
- **Fine Work**
- **Whitest Sneakers**
- **Grace Under Fire**
- **Jim Halpert**
- **Best Dad**
- **Best Mom**
- **Diabetes**
- **Promising Assistant Manager**
- **Cutest Redhead in the Office**
- **Best Dundies Host**
- **Doobie Doobie Pothead Stoner of the Year**
- **Extreme Repulsiveness**
- **Redefining Beauty**
- **Kind of a Bitch**
- **Moving On Up**
- **Worst Salesman of the Year**
- **Great Work**
- **Longest Engagement**
- **Show Me the Money**

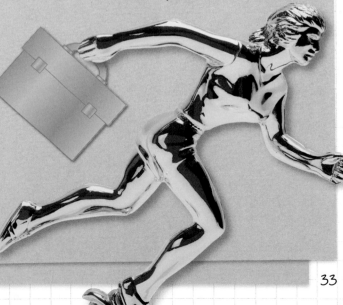

Hosting Gear

Not all venues will allow you to set up a PA system, but it's just not the Dundies without a microphone. So here's a way to craft one yourself. Sure, the mic might not actually work, but if your host is anything like Michael, that's probably for the best.

If for some reason you feel the need to match Michael's formal attire, you can also craft a simple paper bow tie using the below instructions.

BOW TIE SUPPLIES

- ⬇ **Bow Tie Template**
- **Black cardstock**
- **Tape**
- **Scissors**
- **Paper clip**

MICROPHONE SUPPLIES

- **Paper towel tube**
- **2-inch Styrofoam ball**
- **Black and gray acrylic paints**
- **Wooden skewer**
- **Decoupage glue**
- **Silver glitter**
- **Small box**
- **Hot-glue gun**

BOW TIE INSTRUCTIONS

1. Draw the template onto the cardstock, and cut out the bow tie base and collar strip.

2. Fold on the dotted lines to make a perfect bow.

3. Wrap the small rectangle around the bow, and add a small square of tape on the backside.

4. Thread the longer strip into the back, and measure the length around your neck.

5. Paper-clip at the appropriate place, and wear with your favorite collared shirt.

MICROPHONE INSTRUCTIONS

1. Paint the paper towel tube black and the Styrofoam ball gray. While you are waiting for the paint to dry, try out some of your best jokes, and be sure to pause for laughter.

TIP: For painting the ball, use the wooden skewer to keep your fingers out of the paint. This also gives you a way to dry the ball without it touching anything.

2. Once dry, paint a coat of decoupage glue on the Styrofoam, and sprinkle glitter over the ball. Use a small box to contain the glitter. After the initial coat is dry, add a second layer of decoupage glue to seal the glitter.

3. Using the hot-glue gun, attach the ball to the top of the paper towel roll, and run a quick mic check before you hit the stage.

"Every day is 'black tie optional.'"
—Dwight Schrute

"The Dundies are kind of like a kid's birthday party. And you go, and there's really nothing for you to do there. But the kid's having a really good time. So you're kind of there. That's kind of what it's like."
—Oscar Martinez

DUNDIE AWARD
Whitest Sneakers

RECEPTION

DUNDER MIFFLIN, INC.
PAPER COMPANY

"Keep your acceptance speeches short. I have wrap-it-up music, and I'm not afraid to use it . . . Devon."

—Dwight Schrute

DUNDIE AWARDS
NOMINATION CERTIFICATE

IS PRESENTED TO

PAM BEESLY

Of the Scranton branch office for consideration in outstanding
achievement, to be presented an official Dundie Award at a very
Special Evening Ceremony.

DUNDIE AWARD
Whitest Sneakers

Dundie Nomination Certificates

To Michael, the Dundies were on the same level as the Oscars. Since he was never able to convince any celebrities to read out the nominees in a televised press conference, he decided that the next best option was to show up at his staff's homes at completely inappropriate times to hand deliver invitations to the big event.

Feel free to do the same (or just hand them out during office hours). The official Dundie Nomination Certificate Template ⬇ is easy to find on the online resources page. There are instructions here on how to recreate the file from scratch if someone *accidentally* deletes it.

SUPPLIES
- **Computer**
- **Word processing software**
- **Printer**
- **Cardstock in cream, size 8½ by 11 inches**

"Anything can happen at the Dundies. They're like the Golden Globes, but less mean."

—Michael Scott

1. Open the word processing software on your computer.

2. Change the page layout to Landscape. Adjust the page size to 7¾ inches by 9¾ inches

3. Add a border around the outside edge of the page to create a cut line.

4. In your word processing software, select the function that creates text boxes that you can move around and customize. Change the font to Times New Roman and type "Dundie Awards." Insert a second text box following the same instructions, and type "Nomination Certificate."

5. Align the Dundie Awards section to be large across the top of the document. Adjust the size of the Nomination Certificate section to line up directly under "Dundie Awards."

6. Create a new text box, and type "Is Presented To" using the built-in "subtle reference" font style or similar font styling. Align center.

7. Create a new text box with a solid line. Align center.

8. Create a new text box with verbiage about your awards. Align center. You can put your event details in this box to indicate where and when the awards ceremony will be. Alternately, you can copy the official Dundies Nominations text:

   Of The Scranton Branch Office

   For Consideration In Outstanding Achievement

   To Be Presented An Official Dundie Award

   At A Very Special Evening Ceremony

9. Emblazon with your signature on the bottom left and add a logo—such as the Dunder Mifflin logo—on the bottom right.

10. Print on cream cardstock.

FUNTIVITIES

Distribute the Dundies

Once the awards get underway, the host should call up each winner by name and announce which Dundie they've won. Make sure the attendees have an acceptance speech ready in case the award they win is one they're proud to receive (and maybe an alternate speech in case the award is particularly insulting).

Dundie Party Playlist

During transitions between awards, to be especially true to the show, here are the collected "N3P" songs Michael parodied for his Dundie Party Playlist.

- **"Tiny Dancer"**
- **"O.P.P. (You Down with the Dundies)"**
- **"I've Had the Time of My Life"**
- **"You Sexy Thing"**
- **"Seasons of Love"**

DUNDIES DOS AND DON'TS

Once the nominations have been delivered, the trophies have been personalized, and the venue has been secured, there's no turning back. Despite your better judgment, the Dundies are happening. So it's up to you and the other members of your Party Planning Committee to make sure things keep running as smoothly as possible, even when your host starts to veer off the rails. Some tips:

If the Dundies are being presented at a local restaurant chain, aim for one that has a private party room. You may be required to sit through endless hours of inside jokes, but that doesn't mean the entire restaurant should be forced to do the same.

To be true to the show, have a sound system with a mic to be able to play music during and in between awards. If anyone in your office is as musical as Darryl or Andy, maybe offer them a chance to take care of the music.

If a restaurant isn't an option, the show must go on. Host your Dundies in the office's conference room, and decorate the table with a centerpiece of margarita glasses, the cleanest white sneakers,

and a few Dundies from years past. Serve the Sizzling Queso Dip With Chorizo (page 31) and Extra-Awesome Mini Onion Blossoms (page 29) as appetizers. You can even set up the Fajitas (page 28) on a side table to create a self-service fajita bar. Lastly, keep the Second Drink Margaritas (page 31) pouring to liven up the party.

No matter where or how you celebrate, recognizing everyone's valuable contributions to the team is the most important part of the evening!

"I want to thank God. Because God gave me this Dundie. And I feel God in this Chili's tonight."
—Pam Beesly

Office Olympics

As Jim once said, nothing brings out the best in us like the eternal burning of competition. Unlike the real Olympics, which take years of practice and training, the Games of the Dunder Mifflin Olympiad are a loose collection of sports-like challenges that they made up to keep themselves from dying of boredom while filling out expense reports. If your office needs a morale boost, this is your chance to go for the gold. Or silver. Or bronze. (Which are really blue, and they're also the back side of the gold, so no flipping, okay? Honor system.)

Office Olympics Medals

While everyone goes home a winner, not everyone gets first place during the Office Olympics. These award-winning medals are the perfect way to recognize the real MVP of the party.

SUPPLIES
- **Three metal yogurt tops (cleaned)**
- **Gold paint**
- **Silver paint**
- **Blue paint**
- **Paper clips**

INSTRUCTIONS

1. Flatten the yogurt tops as best you can, and when possible, shape them into a round circle.

2. Paint one side of a yogurt top gold, paint the second lid silver, and the third blue. Let dry, and then turn over and paint the lid backs with the corresponding colors.

3. While the tops are drying, begin to assemble your paper clips into a chain. Loop the paper clips together end to end until you have a completed chain measuring approximately 2 feet long. Join the last paper clips in the chain together to create a loop. Repeat two more times for a total of 3 chains.

4. Use a new paper clip to poke a small hole through the gold medal so that the medal hangs from the paper clip. Repeat with the other two medals.

5. Loop the paper clip that is holding the medal onto one of the chains. Repeat twice more.

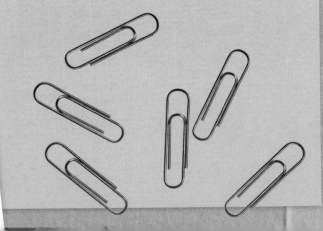

Flonkerton

The national sport of Icelandic paper companies, Flonkerton roughly translates to "box of paper snowshoe racing." That might be because it's a sport where you wear boxes of paper like snowshoes and race. It's just that simple and yet so complex at the same time. Here's how to play:

1. You'll need two full boxes of paper per contestant. It's important that the boxes are still bound by the plastic strapping, also known as "flonks."

2. Each contestant stands on top of the paper boxes and slips the toe of their shoe under the front "flonk."

3. When the race begins, players shuffle forward as fast as possible with the heavy boxes strapped to their feet.

4. The first to cross the finish line gets the gold medal in Flerninton. Flonkerton. Whatever.

Dunderball

The Games of the Dunder Mifflin Olympiad managed to draw competitors from the reception desk to as far away as the annex. It's from that strange and distant land that the game of Dunderball came to be. The rules are simple:

1. Each player sits in their adjacent cubicle, separated by a divider. This game works best when the cubicles are facing a wall.

2. Mark the boundary of each player's side by placing a strip of colored tape on the wall up to the ceiling above the players' cubicles. This helps clearly denote the sides of the Dunderball court.

3. The first player bounces a small rubber ball off the wall on their side of the tape.

4. The other player catches the ball on its rebound. They may hold it for a one second count before bouncing it off their side of the wall to return it.

5. The ball ricochets back and forth between players until someone misses a catch.

6. So, basically, volleyball.

Who can put the most chocolate candies in their mouth?

Everyone knows there ain't no party like a Scranton party! Kick off your Dundies by challenging guests to see who can put the most chocolate candies in their mouth at one time. But don't bother trying too hard for the record. Kevin will never be dethroned.

Award first-, second-, and third-place winners with their Office Olympics Medals (opposite page).

Prank

STAPLER IN GELATIN

Remember when I said that you need to respect other members of the Party Planning Committee? Well, as hard as you might try, that's not always possible. They're going to get under your skin now and then, and rather than throwing a fit or calling names, you might want to take a page out of Jim's book and pull a prank on them instead. Here's one of his favorties that he says will earn you some "big flans." Simply select your favorite—or least favorite—coworker and encase some of their personal effects in the center of a colorful gelatinous dessert. Then, remind them of all the starving people in the world so that their guilt forces them to eat the item free from its sweet suspension. But try not to go overboard with this one. The thing about a practical joke is that you have to know when to start and when to stop. If you take it too far and damage to company property occurs, you may be taken into custard-y.

- **Bowl big enough to submerge stapler with a couple extra inches above**
- **4 envelopes unflavored gelatin**
- **4 cups cold water, divided**
- **Four 3-ounce boxes of lemon-flavored (or other yellow-colored) gelatin**
- **4 cups boiling water, divided**
- **Stapler**

1. In your bowl, sprinkle 1 envelope of unflavored gelatin over 1 cup of cold water, and allow to bloom for 2 minutes.

2. Stir 1 box of lemon gelatin into 1 cup of boiling water until the gelatin has dissolved. Whisk the lemon gelatin into the unflavored gelatin. Refrigerate and allow to set for at least 3 hours, or until completely set. Once the base layer is set, use the remaining 3 envelopes of unflavored gelatin, 3 cups of cold water, 3 boxes of lemon gelatin, and 3 cups of boiling water, following the same process to create more gelatin mixture. Cool to room temperature.

3. Remove the bowl with the base layer from the refrigerator, and place the stapler upside-down into the gelatin. You may have to press the stapler into the gelatin a bit to get it to stay in the position you want. Make sure the stapler is set fully below the rim of the bowl but not pushing all the way through the base layer. Fill with the gelatin mixture, return to the refrigerator, and allow to set overnight.

4. To unmold, set the bowl in hot water for about a minute, run an offset spatula around the edge, and place a plate (large enough to cover the bowl) on top of the bowl and flip.

Wedding Shower

"Webster's Dictionary defines 'wedding' as 'the fusing of two metals with a hot torch.' Well, you know something? I think you guys are two medals. Gold medals."

—Michael Scott

Although office romances aren't usually condoned by HR, sometimes corporate policies aren't enough to stop a friendship between coworkers from blossoming into something more. Once a ring is placed on a finger, it's the Party Planning Committee's chance to shine by throwing an epic wedding shower that the happy couple will never forget. While it may not be quite as special as the wedding day itself, there's a good chance that this will be the second most important day of their lives. Or at least top twenty.

If you're throwing a wedding shower at the office, it obviously doesn't need to be as formal as the actual ceremony, but you should still show respect for the couple by dressing nicely for the occasion. As Michael insisted on the show, no one should look like a ragamuffin, so get your suit to the dry cleaner, get your hair did, and invest in a dress or a skirt of some kind if you don't already have one. It should go without saying, wearing tissue boxes instead of shoes is a major faux pas!

One more important thing: When picking a present for the happy couple, try to give it a bit more thought than your basic office gift exchange. They might ask for cash only, but according to Michael, since they get a paycheck from the company every week, that seems a little repetitive. Instead, go with something they might actually need in their new life together, like a toaster. But if you're determined to do something special and original, try painting a portrait of the couple from memory. If that doesn't work out, every new couple needs a set of turtle boiling pots and shell hammers.

FUN TIP:

The more the merrier! Usually a wedding shower is "ladies only," but we all saw how that played out during Phyllis's shower. It might be in everyone's best interest to keep an eye on the men. If they aren't impressed by the awesome spread you have planned, they'll definitely be won over by the poker game you set up in the corner. The more all-inclusive fun you offer, the less likely they'll be to care that you didn't hire any strippers. Well, maybe the Packer of your office will care, but anytime he's disappointed it's usually a win for everyone else.

Scrantonicity Sliders

Since most guests come to a wedding only for the food and entertainment, why not combine the best of both at the wedding shower? These sliders steal the show with a spicy relish that is guaranteed to get everyone sweating on the dance floor. So what if the band has played only three weddings before? You'll want to book these sliders not just for your next wedding shower but for every party you throw!

Prep Time: 5 minutes
Cook Time: 30 minutes
Yield: 10 sliders

13 slices bacon, divided
2 pounds lean ground beef
Salt and black pepper, to taste
5 slices sharp cheddar cheese, cut in half
½ cup Spicy and Sweet Red Pepper Relish (page 128)
10 slider buns

1. In a large skillet over medium-high heat, cook 8 slices of bacon until cooked through but not crispy, about 5 minutes. Remove from the pan, and place on a paper towel–lined plate to drain and allow to cool. Once cool, chop the bacon into small pieces.

2. Cook the other 5 slices of bacon until crispy, about 8 minutes, and remove from the pan to a paper towel–lined plate to drain and cool, and then cut in half. Set aside, and clean most of the bacon fat from the skillet.

3. In a large bowl, combine the ground beef and chopped bacon. Season the meat mixture with salt and pepper. Form into 10 bite-size patties. Place a skillet over medium heat, and cook the patties in batches, about 6 minutes on each side for medium and 7 to 8 minutes for well-done. During the last 2 minutes of cooking, place a piece of cheese on each, and cover the pan to melt the cheese.

4. Put one slider on the bottom of each slider bun, and then lay one piece of cooked bacon on each. Add a scant tablespoon of hot pepper relish, and top with the other bun. Serve.

"No, this is not our first wedding. This is the third wedding that Scrantonicity has played. We also played our bassist's wedding and our guitarist's wedding."

—Kevin Malone

Meemaw's Baby Vegetable Salad

If you want to serve something traditional at your wedding shower, Meemaw has you covered. Her roasted baby vegetables with herb-shallot vinaigrette are time-tested and sure to please guests of all ages. Of course, you may want a plan B. Meemaw is as old-fashioned as they come, so she might not allow any talk of babies before the wedding. Even of the vegetable variety.

Prep Time: 10 minutes
Yield: 4 servings

FOR THE HERB-SHALLOT VINAIGRETTE:

1 small shallot, peeled and cut in half
2 tablespoons fresh parsley
3 tablespoons fresh basil
2 teaspoons Dijon mustard
Juice of ½ a lemon
⅔ cup olive oil
½ cup white wine vinegar
Salt and black pepper, to taste

FOR THE SALAD:

4 cups (from a 5-ounce bag) baby kale
One 14-ounce can artichoke hearts, roughly chopped
One 15-ounce can baby corn spears, roughly chopped
4 baby zucchini, sliced into rounds
1 cup grape tomatoes
1 cup crumbled feta cheese

1. Prepare the vinaigrette. Combine the shallot, herbs, and mustard in a food processor fit with a chopping blade. Pulse a few times to loosely chop the ingredients. In a bowl, combine the lemon juice, olive oil, and white wine vinegar. Turn the food processor on high, and while the machine is running, slowly pour in the liquids. Pouring should be very slow and take at least 30 seconds. When the dressing is totally emulsified (completely combined), turn off the food processor, and add salt and pepper to taste. Pour the dressing into a bowl or bottle, and set aside.

2. In a large salad bowl, combine the salad ingredients. Dress to taste with vinaigrette, toss, and serve.

Champagne Cupcakes

Ice-cream cake might seem appropriate for just about any office party, but a wedding shower calls for a more elegant dessert option. While the wedding cake might not be ready to cut quite yet, these miniature versions should prove a suitable substitute. Hopefully, the day doesn't go by too quickly and you're lucky enough to enjoy a few of these delightful desserts.

Prep Time: 20 minutes
Cook Time: 20 minutes
Yield: 24 cupcakes

FOR THE CUPCAKES:

4 egg whites, room temperature
1½ cups sugar
1 cup (2 sticks) salted butter, room temperature
2½ cups all-purpose flour
2 teaspoons baking powder
½ teaspoon baking soda
1 cup champagne

FOR THE CHAMPAGNE BUTTERCREAM FROSTING:

½ cup (1 stick) salted butter, room temperature
4 cups confectioners' sugar
¼ cup plus 2 tablespoons champagne
Gold food coloring spray, optional

1. Preheat the oven to 350°F. Line two 12-cupcake baking pans with paper liners.

2. Prepare the cupcakes. In the bowl of a stand mixer fitted with a balloon whisk, beat the egg whites on low until they're frothy, and then on high until they form stiff peaks, about 5 minutes. Remove the egg whites to a medium bowl, and let rest in the refrigerator until needed.

3. Fit the mixer with a flat beater, and using the same bowl, combine the sugar and butter on medium-high until very creamy, about 4 to 5 minutes.

4. In a medium bowl, combine the flour, baking powder, and baking soda.

5. Lower the mixer speed to medium-low, and then add ¼ of the dry mixture, followed by ¼ of the champagne. Continue, alternating wet and dry, until fully incorporated.

6. Remove the bowl from the mixer, and take the egg whites from the refrigerator. Using a rubber spatula, incorporate ⅓ of the egg whites into the batter by gently folding them in, taking care not to overmix or flatten the egg whites. Repeat two more times with the remaining egg whites.

7. Divide evenly among the cupcake liners. Bake for 18 to 20 minutes, rotating the pan once halfway through to ensure even baking. Check doneness by inserting a toothpick or knife into the center of a cupcake. If it comes out clean, cupcakes are ready. Remove from the oven, and allow to cool completely.

8. Prepare the buttercream. In the bowl of a stand mixer fitted with a flat beater, cream the butter and sugar on medium-high until light and fluffy. Reduce the speed to low, and slowly incorporate the champagne.

9. Transfer the frosting to a pastry bag fitted with a large star tip, and pipe a generous swirl of frosting onto each cupcake. Finish with a light mist of the gold food coloring spray, if using. Top with crafted Cupcake Toppers (page 54).

"They say that your wedding day goes by in such a flash that you're lucky if you even get a piece of your own cake. I say that's crazy. I say, 'Let them eat cake.' Margaret Thatcher said that about marriage. Smart broad."

—Michael Scott

Niagara Falls Mimosa

When Jim and Pam got married, they invited all of their friends from the office up to Niagara Falls to attend the ceremony. But things got a little crazy, so they snuck out and secretly got married on a boat without telling anyone. This sparkling cocktail is beautiful and light, which is exactly how they felt that day, and it's the perfect way to celebrate anyone getting ready to take the plunge.

Prep Time: 5 minutes
Yield: 1 serving

½ ounce blue curaçao
Brut sparkling wine
Lemon twist

1. Pour the blue curaçao into a champagne flute. Fill the glass three-quarters full with sparkling wine.

2. Garnish with a lemon twist, and serve.

"I live by one rule: No office romances, no way. Very messy, inappropriate . . . no. But, I live by another rule: Just do it . . ."

—Michael Scott

CRAFTS

Dos and Don'ts

Wedding etiquette is important, and if you're planning on inviting your coworkers, it's something that needs to be discussed well before the big day arrives—at least it needed to be at the Scranton branch. The wedding shower is the perfect opportunity to lay the ground rules. Put the conference room's whiteboard to good use and draft a quick list of Dos and Don'ts. Some may seem like common sense, but as you know, that's never something to take for granted. You may have different ideas than the ones from Jim and Pam's wedding, but it's still probably smart to keep firecrackers in the "don't" column, just in case.

SUPPLIES
- **Whiteboard**
- **Dry-erase markers**

1. Divide the board in two sections. Write "Do" at the top of one section and "Don't" at the top of the other.

2. Write out a comprehensive list of what guests should and should not do at the wedding. Make sure to take the bride and groom's personal preferences into account, while inserting a few inside jokes about the happy couple that everyone will enjoy. Jim and Pam's original list is included to the right for your reference.

> Wedding Rules
>
> **Do**
> Have a good time
> Dance when _appropriate_
> Eat dinner
>
> **Don't**
> Make a big scene
> Cry   VERY
> Talk to our family BUSY
> Firecrackers

"This is supposed to be our wedding day. Why did we invite all these people?"

—Pam Beesly

"The best wedding I've ever been to. I got six numbers. One more would have been a complete telephone number."

—Kevin Malone

Tissue Box Shoes

Although he wasn't a member of the Party Planning Committee, Dunder Mifflin's resident accountant and drummer, Kevin Malone, had a handy tip in the event of a footwear foul-up during the festivities:

"Weddings need shoes. But sometimes you send your shoes to get shined and the hotel staff incinerates them instead. That's not good. But a lack of proper footwear shouldn't stop you from hitting the dance floor—not when your hotel has free boxes of tissues in the lobby. These makeshift shoes aren't the most comfortable things you've ever worn, but I promise they'll be a huge conversation piece."

SUPPLIES

- **2 large tissue boxes**

1. Open tissue boxes.

2. Remove tissues.

3. Place boxes on feet.

4. Wear all day.

TIP: This was Kevin's questionable follow-up to the footwear foul-up: "If your dogs are barking from the poor arch support provided by your tissue box shoes, just pop them into the hotel ice machine to reduce any pain or swelling. Don't worry, your feet will probably be so sweaty you won't even feel the cold!"

Wedding Attire

While a couple always remembers what they wore on their wedding day, it shouldn't overshadow the true meaning of the celebration. When Pam tore her veil, she was almost convinced that her perfect day was ruined. But Jim came to her rescue, as he always does, and cut his tie in half, reminding her that how they were dressed was only a small part of the puzzle. This craft is a special way to commemorate that moment and help future couples remember that the only perfect thing they need on their wedding day is their love.

SUPPLIES
- **Bridal veil**
- **Necktie**
- **Scissors**

WEDDING ATTIRE INSTRUCTIONS

1. In a noticeable area of the veil, tear a rip where everyone will see.

2. While wearing the tie, cut it in half with scissors a few inches below the knot.

3. Wear the veil and tie together during the shower as a reminder that the wedding is about the couple and not about the decorations.

Painted Portrait

Michael always believed that a wedding gift has to come from the heart, which is why he gave Jim and Pam a portrait he admittedly painted from memory. He also admitted he did a draft of them in the nude, as well. It should go without saying that you probably shouldn't do that, and if you do, definitely don't tell the couple you did.

SUPPLIES
- **Large canvas**
- **Acrylic paint**
- **Paintbrushes**

1. Set the scene for the painting with a beautiful backdrop. Michael's portrait featured a sunset behind Jim and Pam. You can do this by painting bands of purple, then pink, then orange across the page. Follow this with a heavy layer of blue for the water. Allow this to dry before painting the ground and the sun with rays of pink emanating from it. Allow the backdrop to dry completely.

2. Paint the happy couple holding hands. Although you can also paint it from memory, it may not hurt to use a reference photo.

Cupcake Toppers

A wedding shower is a time to celebrate the people you love the most. In this case, that was only supposed to mean the future couple, but if your HR manager is anything like Toby, he or she may force you, in the interest of equality, to make a topper for everyone in the office whether they are getting married or not. So when you're making these adorable photo cupcake toppers of the happy couple for your dessert display, you could also use your company resources to make some that look like the night watchman or that guy who you're not entirely sure what he does.

SUPPLIES

- **Glue stick**
- **Printed photos of the bridal party, roughly 2 inches tall**
- **Cardstock**
- **Scissors**
- **Hot-glue gun**
- **Appetizer sticks or toothpicks**

1. Using the glue stick, firmly attach the photos to cardstock.

2. With a pair of scissors, cut the person you wish to feature out of the photo.

3. Use a hot-glue gun to attach the backside of the photo to an appetizer stick.

4. Display alongside your desserts at the party!

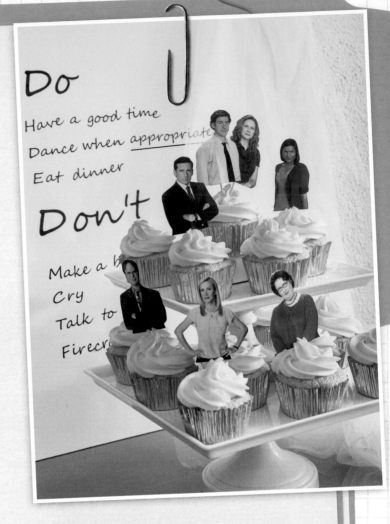

Do
Have a good time
Dance when appropriate
Eat dinner

Don't
Make a b
Cry
Talk to
Firecr

"Since I pay her salary, it is like I am paying for the wedding. Which I'm happy to do. It's a big day for Phyllis, but it's an even bigger day for me. Employer of the bride."

—Michael Scott

"Bride 2 Be" or "Groom 2 Be" Sash

Make sure everyone knows who your guest of honor is by crafting a "Bride 2 Be" or "Groom 2 Be" sash. Phyllis wore one at her bridal shower, and it was a great way to help her feel special and loved in the lead-up to her big day. But beware: If anyone has planned any "entertainment," you could be making the guest of honor a clear target. It doesn't matter if they're booked from a local strip club or the Scholastic Speakers of Pennsylvania because in a case like that, your well-intentioned sash could draw all the wrong kinds of attention.

SUPPLIES

- **3-inch-wide white ribbon**
- **Scissors**
- **Hot-glue gun**
- **Iron-on letters and numbers**
- **Plastic flowers**

1. Cut a piece of ribbon that is approximately 6 feet long.

2. Using yourself or someone who is roughly the same height as the bride-to-be, wrap the sash around your shoulder with the midpoint of the ribbon at your shoulder, and hold the sash at a diagonal across your body. Mark where the sash hits your hip with a pencil or pin.

3. Take off the sash, and fold it so you can see your marking. Glue to fasten the end of the ribbon together, and cut off any excess at the bottom.

4. Using an iron on low, iron on the words "Bride 2 Be" or "Groom 2 Be" across the middle of the sash.

5. Use a hot-glue gun to add a few flowers to the sash to give it the perfect finishing touches. Make sure not to use too many flowers or flowers that are very heavy, as they may affect the balance of the sash.

Tulle Bows

Tulle and weddings go together like Robert Dunder and Robert Mifflin. You can use these tulle bows as decorations or to top a gift for a couple whose relationship is one you have much better knowledge of.

SUPPLIES

- **Cardboard**
- **Scissors**
- **Lightweight tulle**
- **Hot-glue gun**

1. Cut the cardboard into an 8-by-6-inch rectangle.

2. Wrap the tulle around the wide 8-inch side 10 times, and then cut the end of the tulle.

3. Cut a smaller piece of tulle, about 6 inches long.

4. Bunch the tulle together on the cardboard, and being careful to hold on to the middle of the tulle so you don't lose the tulle's shape, slide the tulle off the cardboard.

5. Use the small piece of tulle to tie a tight knot in the middle. Add a dab of hot glue to the knot to keep it together. Let it dry.

6. Cut the looped sides with the scissors, and fluff out the bow.

7. Repeat for more tulle bows to decorate or use on the top of a present.

Flower Crown

Phyllis was ahead of the trends when she wore a flower crown to her wedding. Be a trendsetter and whip one up for the betrothed at their shower.

SUPPLIES
- **Floral wire**
- **Wire cutters**
- **Floral tape**
- **Faux flowers**
- **Faux greenery**
- **Hot-glue gun**

1. Create a base for the crown by cutting a length of floral wire that will wrap around your head or the head of the bride three times.

2. Loop the wire once around to the approximate size of your head, and wrap the remaining wire around the loop, twisting as you go. When you come to the end, use floral tape to tightly secure the edge of the wire.

3. If working with a bunch of faux flowers, cut off the individual flower elements. If they have wires, use those to wrap around the base. If not, attach floral wire to the blooms with floral tape.

4. Continue adding flowers around the wire base until it is properly filled with flowers.

5. Repeat step 3 with greenery, and fill in any areas that look a bit empty to ensure the crown is properly full.

"I'm trying to get everyone excited about Phyllis's wedding, because I want her to get people excited about my wedding, when the time comes. Which won't be hard. Because it's gonna be awesome."

—Michael Scott

1

2

3

4

FUNTIVITIES

Wedding Toast Fill-In Game

Michael could always be counted on to make a toast no matter the celebration when he was specifically asked not to. If you have someone like that in your life, instead of worrying about the words that might come out of their mouth, why not work as a team to craft the perfect toast together? There's no guarantee that anyone will stay on script when the big day comes, but at least you tried!

Start with these templates that are based on toasts from the show, one given by Jim at his rehearsal dinner and the other given by Michael at Phyllis's wedding. See if you can tell which one is which. It really shouldn't be too hard. Then ask your coworkers to provide you with suggestions for the blanks in the following speeches without giving them information about the larger speech as a guide. When you've gathered the best suggestions from the group, read through the newly written speech at the party and decide if it's a winner for the wedding reception.

"_____ years ago, I was just a _____
(Number)   (Noun)
who had a crush on a _____ who had a
                              (Noun)

_____. And I had to do the _____
(Noun)   (Adjective)
thing I've ever had to do, which was to _____.
                                                   (Verb)

And don't get me wrong, I _____ with her . . .
                              (Verb that ends in "ed")

I just had little moments with a _____ who saw
                                          (Noun)

me as a _____. And a lot of people told me I
            (Noun)

was _____ to wait this long for a date with a
         (Adjective)

_____ who I worked with, but I think that even
(Noun)

then I knew that . . . I was waiting for my_____."
                                                      (Noun)

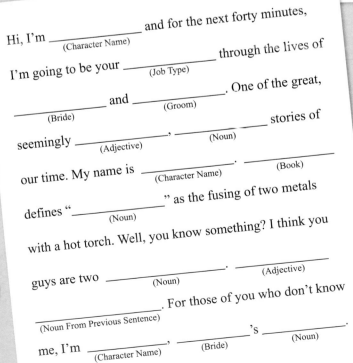

Hi, I'm _____ and for the next forty minutes,
              (Character Name)

I'm going to be your _____ through the lives of
                              (Job Type)

_____ and _____. One of the great,
(Bride)   (Groom)

seemingly _____, _____ stories of
               (Adjective)   (Noun)

our time. My name is _____. _____
                            (Character Name)   (Book)

defines "_____" as the fusing of two metals
              (Noun)

with a hot torch. Well, you know something? I think you

guys are two _____. _____
                      (Noun)   (Adjective)

_____. For those of you who don't know
(Noun From Previous Sentence)

me, I'm _____, _____'s _____.
              (Character Name)   (Bride)   (Noun)

"The Schrutes have their own traditions. We usually marry standing in our own graves. It makes the funerals very romantic, but the weddings are a bleak affair."

—Dwight Schrute

Poker Game

If the guest of honor wants to keep things more traditional and refuses an all-inclusive wedding shower, then don't be surprised if the excluded plan their own "Afternoon In." In order to keep things corporate friendly, you can help set up all the distraction they'll need with a rousing game of poker. All you need is a table, a deck of cards, and if you have them, a set of poker chips. Hopefully, it will keep them busy enough that they stay out of trouble.

"It's a bridal shower for guys. A guy shower. An hour-long shower with guys."

—Michael Scott

HOW WELL DO YOU KNOW THE HAPPY COUPLE?

1. Who is the bride's favorite Dunder Mifflin employee?

2. What kind of paper would the groom order? Regular or three-hole punch?

3. Who is the bride's favorite historical character?

4. What Halloween costume will the couple wear next year?

5. Where was the couple's first kiss?

How Well Do You Know the Happy Couple?

Games are a trademark of a fun wedding shower celebration. Since all the guests know the happy couple in some capacity, pass out a sheet with some questions about them, and see how the answers match up to the ones you asked the couple before the event. If you ask the right questions, the game can be a lot of fun. After all, it's one thing to quiz a Ben Franklin impersonator on who the king of Austria, Prussia, or England is, and it's a completely other kind of fun to ask him about his girlfriends in Paris or if he wears boxers, briefs, or pantaloons!

DÉCOR

Wedding showers are formal and elegant and should showcase the love the couple shares. Gather photos of the couple together, and display them throughout the shower in silver and gold frames picked up at your local discount store.

If you know the wedding's color palette, use that to inspire your decorations. Create centerpieces using the same kind of flowers that you used in the bride's flower crown, drape the tables with tulle, and add Tulle Bows (page 55) to tables or chairs to bring an additional layer of class to the gathering. Be sure to give the bride her Flower Crown (page 56) and "Bride 2 Be" or "Groom 2 Be" Sash (page 55) when the guest of honor arrives.

Top the Champagne Cupcakes (page 48) with the Cupcake Toppers (page 54), and set them on a table with Scrantonicity Sliders (page 46), Meemaw's Baby Vegetable Salad (page 47), and the Niagara Falls Mimosas (page 50). Set the Dos and Don'ts List (page 51) nearby, and if you've created a Painted Portrait (page 53) place it somewhere visible to create a real conversation starter.

PRANK

Hiring a stripper may seem like Bachelor and Bachelorette Party 101, but a wedding shower calls for something a bit more sophisticated. Instead of hiring someone in the buff, why not go with a history buff instead? When Michael handed Jim the reins to book the entertainment for Phyllis's shower, he hired a local reenactor, thinking it would be a great prank. But the joke was on him, because it actually ended up being surprisingly fun and educational. That is, until Ben Franklin ended up hitting on Pam . . . so ultimately the joke really was on . . . everyone?

Baby Shower

> "Jan is about to have a baby with a sperm donor. And Michael is preparing for the birth of a watermelon with Dwight. Now, this baby will be related to Michael through . . . delusion."
>
> —Jim Halpert

There's nothing more worthy of celebration than the act of bringing a new life into the world. We're all familiar with the age-old concept of *What to Expect When You're Expecting*, but when the person who is pregnant happens to be one of your coworkers, then what they should expect before they head to the delivery room is one awesome party!

In many cases, this is your chance to show a mother-to-be what they mean to the office before they depart for months of maternity leave, so it's important to leave a lasting impression. No one expects live storks, but a few balloons and some bowls of candy aren't enough to make the cut. As Michael would say, if you're going to throw a shower, you have to make it golden! It may take some extra work, but it will be a labor of love.

While the majority of office parties are actually no more than excuses for coworkers to drink together, baby showers require a totally different type of distraction (at least for the guest of honor). That's where party games come in! Join the fun by guessing when the baby will be born, identifying your office mates by their baby pictures, or tying a stroller to your car's bumper to test its safety features. Fun for all ages!

> "I do not like pregnant women in my workspace. They're always complaining. I have varicose veins too. I have swollen ankles. I'm constantly hungry. You think my nipples don't get sore too? Do you think I don't need to know the fastest way to the hospital?"
>
> —Stanely Hudson

FUN TIP:

Be ready to adapt. Due dates aren't set in stone, so you never know when a shower designed to celebrate someone's impending motherhood will suddenly need to pivot to celebrate the fact that they've already been a mother for weeks—and never bothered to tell anyone. While an unexpected early arrival certainly might disrupt some of the games and activities you worked so hard to plan, don't let it ruin the day. After all, a baby multiplies the fun! And at least you'll have an extra guest of honor to celebrate, which is especially helpful if you weren't a huge fan of the original guest of honor to begin with . . .

Scott's Loaded Tater Tots

Baby showers are about more than just the day of the party. They're about the future and all the potential it holds. It's so easy to get carried away in all the emotion of the moment, but remember, this day isn't about you. Grand gestures, like promising to pay the baby's college tuition, are unnecessary when you could simply bring an amazing appetizer like this one.

This recipe includes directions to make tater tots from scratch, but you can always just use store-bought frozen tater tots.

Prep Time: 15 minutes
Cook Time: 35 minutes
Yield: 4 servings as an appetizer or side

FOR THE TATER TOTS:

Olive oil cooking spray
2 pounds russet potatoes, peeled and diced
1 tablespoon cornstarch
1 teaspoon black pepper
1 teaspoon salt
2 teaspoons onion powder
2 teaspoons garlic powder
2 tablespoons chopped chives, fresh or dried

FOR SCOTT'S LOADED TATER TOTS:

36 tater tots, premade or from this recipe
½ cup bacon, cooked and crumbled (about 8 slices)
1 medium tomato, diced
¼ cup scallions, tender green and white parts only, sliced into rounds
2 cups shredded cheese, such as cheddar or mozzarella
Salsa and sour cream, as garnish

1. Preheat the oven to 450°F. Line a baking sheet with foil, and spray the foil generously with olive oil cooking spray.

2. Prepare the tots. Bring a medium pot of water to a boil over high heat. Add the potatoes, and boil until just tender, about 15 minutes. Drain the potatoes, and rinse in a colander under cold water. Allow to drain thoroughly.

3. Shred the potatoes in a food processor and then transfer to a medium bowl, or roughly mash them in a bowl by hand with a potato masher. Mix in remaining ingredients. Form into tot-shaped cylinders, and place onto the baking sheet. Spray generously with olive oil spray.

4. Bake for 20 to 25 minutes until golden brown on all sides, rotating frequently to ensure even browning. Remove from the oven, and reduce heat to 400°F.

5. Transfer the tots to a 9-by-13-inch baking dish that has been lightly greased with additional olive oil cooking spray. Sprinkle the bacon, tomatoes, and scallions over the tots, and cover with cheese.

6. Bake until the cheese is melted, 8 to 10 minutes. Remove from the oven, top with salsa and sour cream, and serve.

Watermelon and Feta Salad

Did someone bring a well-buttered watermelon into the office to simulate the wonders of the birthing process? Well, once his disturbing display is over, there's no need to let all that fruit go to waste. Just dice that melon as part of this cool, refreshing salad. Use a permanent marker to secretly tag your plate in a way that only you can recognize and no salad snatcher could ever copy.

Prep Time: 10 minutes
Yield: 8 servings

8 cups watermelon, cubed
½ cup fresh mint, chopped
**6 ounces feta cheese, from a block
(not prepackaged crumbles)**
¼ cup olive oil
Juice of 1 lime
Salt and black pepper, to taste

1. In a large bowl, combine the watermelon and mint. Crumble the feta over the mixture, and stir gently to combine.

2. Drizzle the olive oil and lime juice over the salad, and season with salt and pepper. Serve immediately.

NOTE: You can easily customize this to your own taste by adding cucumber or red onion, or serving everything over a base of greens, like baby arugula. Don't prep this salad in advance, though—the watermelon softens very quickly when mixed with the other ingredients.

"Jan had the baby, and Michael wasn't there to mark it. So the baby could be anybody's. Except Michael's."

—Dwight Schrute

Ultra-Feast
Macaroni and Cheese

Bring on the Ultra Feast! If your shower's "mom of honor" has had an increased appetite during her final months of pregnancy, why not skip second breakfast, lunch, second lunch, and first dinner, and roll it all together into one giant Ultra-Feast? This massive meal is the perfect chance for you to pig out together in the name of ceremony! So grab a fork, start cooking, and get your shower on!

Prep Time: 10 minutes
Cook Time: 1 hour 45 minutes
Yield: 4 to 6 servings as a main, 8 to 10 servings as a side dish

FOR THE MAC AND CHEESE:

½ cup (1 stick) salted butter
¼ cup all-purpose flour
1 teaspoon garlic powder
1 teaspoon onion powder
1½ teaspoons mustard powder
1½ teaspoons paprika
4 cups whole milk, room temperature
One 12-ounce can evaporated milk
3 cups freshly grated mozzarella or cheddar cheese
2 cups freshly grated Gruyère or Parmesan cheese
1 pound elbow macaroni or medium shell pasta
Salt and black pepper, to taste

FOR THE ULTRA FEAST:

2 cups cooked, shredded chicken
2 cups baby spinach
6 slices bacon, cooked and crumbled
½ cup hot sauce, or more to taste

1. Turn on a slow cooker to low.

2. Make the roux: In a large saucepan over medium heat, melt the butter, and then whisk in the flour, garlic powder, onion powder, dry mustard, and paprika. Cook, whisking continuously until the mixture is golden brown and the dry ingredients are completely combined, about 15 minutes.

3. Still whisking, slowly stir in the liquids. (Adding the liquids too fast, or neglecting to bring the milk to room temperature before you do this step, will cause the mixture to curdle.) Bring back up to a simmer. Whisk in the cheeses, and stir until they melt into a smooth sauce.

"I need a baby. I'll never outsell Jim and Pam without one. Also, I've been noticing a gaping hole in my life. Sometimes I wake up cradling a gourd."

—Dwight Schrute

4. Empty the uncooked pasta into the slow cooker, and pour the cheese sauce over the pasta. Stir to combine, and season to taste with salt and pepper.

5. Cook on low for about 90 minutes, stirring every 20 minutes, until the pasta is tender. For the Ultra-Feast version, stir in the extra ingredients in the last 15 minutes of cooking. Keep warm on the lowest setting until ready to serve.

NOTE: This mac and cheese uses a slow cooker and is perfect to bring to a work potluck. It's tempting to use pre-shredded cheese for its convenience, but that won't melt as well as freshly grated cheese, and will prevent the sauce from becoming smooth.

The Astird and the Chevy

Is it a boy or a girl? Your shower's decorations may depend on that sensitive information, but some parents-to-be prefer to keep the gender a secret. If that's the case, there's still a way to use the mystery to your advantage. Just mix up two cocktails, one pink and one blue, and christen them with the potential names for the impending arrival. (As always, be sure to check spelling!)

THE ASTIRD:

Prep Time: 5 minutes
Yield: 1 serving

1 cup granulated sugar
3 sprigs fresh mint
2 lime wedges, plus more for garnish
3 strawberries, plus more for garnish
2 ounces botanical gin
Club soda
Fresh mint, for garnish

1. Prepare the simple syrup: In a small saucepan, combine the sugar and mint with 1 cup of water. Bring to a boil, stirring so that the sugar dissolves completely. Remove from the heat, and allow to cool completely. Strain the simple syrup, discarding the mint.

2. In a highball or pint glass, squeeze the lime wedges to release their juices, and then add the strawberries and ½ ounce simple syrup. Muddle with a spoon until the fruit is mostly broken down. Add the gin.

3. Fill the glass with ice, and fill to the top with club soda. Stir to mix, and garnish with a sprig of mint, additional strawberries, and another lime wedge.

THE CHEVY:

Prep Time: 5 minutes
Yield: 1 serving

2 lemon wedges, divided
8 blueberries, plus more for garnish
½ ounce blue curaçao
2 ounces botanical gin
Club soda

1. In a highball or pint glass, squeeze one lemon wedge to release the juice, and then add the blueberries. Muddle with a spoon until the fruit is mostly broken down. Add the blue curaçao and gin.

2. Fill the glass with ice, and fill to the top with club soda. Stir to mix, and garnish with a lemon wedge and a few blueberries.

"Don't get too hung up on baby names. I was named Walter Jr., after my father, until I was about six or so, when my parents changed their minds."

—Andy Bernard

CRAFTS

Baby Shower Banner

Every mother-to-be deserves to know how much her coworkers adore her. (Or, in some cases, tolerate her presence for eight hours a day.) A shower is a wonderful way to show your support as well as your eagerness to meet the newest member of your office family.

Since Scranton didn't have a pet store with live storks (and you probably don't either), the next best option is a beautiful baby shower banner that welcomes everyone to the fun.

SUPPLIES

- **Scissors**
- **Cardstock in blue, pink, or gender-neutral colors**
- **Hole punch**
- **Marker**
- **Thin ribbon**

1. Cut at least 11 isosceles triangles that are about 9 inches tall and 4 inches wide from cardstock. An easy way to do this is to cut out a template, and then use the template to trace out additional triangles onto a piece of cardstock. Then, stack no more than 2 or 3 sheets of cardstock together and cut along the template lines to get matching triangles. Repeat until you have enough triangles. Use gender-neutral colors such as yellow and green, or alternate blue and pink. Feel free to cut additional triangles to increase the size of your banner.

2. Punch 1 hole in the bottom corners (the short edge) of each of the triangles.

3. Use large block letters to write or cut out the letters in a different color of cardstock to spell "BABY SHOWER" across the triangles, reserving a blank triangle for the space. Each triangle should showcase 1 letter.

4. Cut a piece of ribbon that is long enough to fit all the triangles you'd like to have on the banner. Lay out the triangles in order, making sure to have an equal number of extra blank triangles on either side of the letters, if using. String the triangles on the ribbon in order.

Diaper Banner

As adorable as it is, this banner is sure to serve as a harsh reminder of all the diapers that parents will be changing once their new bundle of joy arrives on the scene. There's a template for this banner on the online resources page, but if you run out of time to craft fake diapers, just purchase a box of disposables and use clothespins to hang them from the ribbon instead.

SUPPLIES

- **Computer**
- ⬇ **Diaper Banner Template**
- **Printer**
- **Cardstock**
- **Scissors**
- **Decorative safety pins**
- **Ribbon**

1. Use your computer and printer to print out 10 diaper templates from the online resources page on cardstock. Use scissors to cut out each template. If you have access to a cutting machine, use the SVG file. You can also cut by hand, but remember to add the cuts in the diaper back, as these will be used to attach the diapers to the banner.

2. Fold the bottom of the diaper up and the sides in. Attach with tape on the inside of the diaper. Do not flatten.

3. Pin a decorative safety pin through the front of the paper diaper.

4. Slide the ribbon through the precut holes in the back to display.

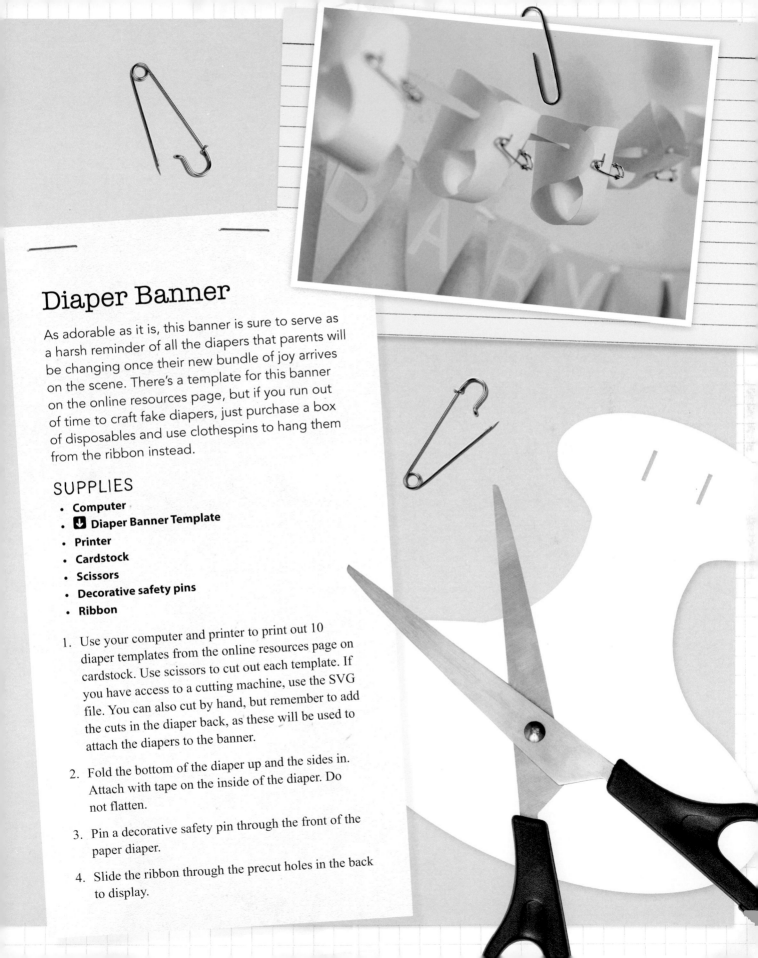

Mom's or Dad's Throne

The new mom or dad deserves a seat of honor throughout the party. This throne creates the perfect backdrop for photos and provides a dedicated place for him or her to take a break when needed.

SUPPLIES
- **2 large yellow poster boards**
- **Packing tape**
- **Chair**
- **Pencil**
- **Scissors**
- **Sticky notes in yellow, pink, and blue**

1. Use packing tape to tape the poster boards together to create an extra-wide piece of poster board as the basis for the back for your throne. You can overlap the pieces of poster board by an inch or two to add a little additional strength before taping.

2. Measure the height and width of the poster board against the back of the chair you wish to use for the parent-to-be, and mark the poster board in pencil so you have a guide as to how large you need to make the design.

3. Draw the top of the throne with pencil, and cut out the arches. You can make it as decorative or as simple as you'd like, but make sure it will be larger than the chairback and frame the parent-to-be.

4. Cover the throne back with sticky notes, using yellow as the primary color. Add blue and pink trim where appropriate.

5. Before the party, slide the back onto the chair and attach with tape. Add sticky notes down the arms of the chair to complete the look.

"Twelve hundred dollars is what I spent on my whole bomb shelter. For that kind of money, this stroller should be indestructible."

—Dwight Schrute

Office Baby Photo Board

Games are an obligatory part of a baby shower, but they don't have to be boring. In fact, with some help from your coworkers, they can be pretty hilarious! Asking everyone in the office to provide a baby photo of themselves ahead of time is the perfect way to create the centerpiece of an activity that will keep everyone engaged and excited. For instructions on how to play, go to the Funtivities on the next page.

SUPPLIES
- **Photos of guests as babies**
- **Cardstock**
- **Glue stick**
- **Trifold display board**
- **Baby shower stickers**
- **Pen**

1. At least two weeks prior to the party, request baby photos from the guests attending and the family of the parents. Be sure to clarify that people should send in copies of the photos, as you don't want to destroy a priceless photo. Alternately, ask coworkers to send photos digitally and then print them yourself.

2. Cut colored frames from cardstock, and attach the photos to the frames with a glue stick.

3. Attach each provided photo to the trifold display board, and embellish with stickers.

4. Number the photos.

"Babies are drawn to me. And I think it's because they see me as one of them. But cooler. And with my life put together a little bit."

—Michael Scott

FUNTIVITIES

Guess the Baby

Once you've gathered your coworkers' baby pictures and created a photo board (page 73), provide the guests with paper for them to write down their guesses as to who's who. This game can be set up prior to the party's start so that people can make their way over to the game as the party gets underway.

Ask everyone to make their guesses as the party gets rolling, and once the Funtivities get started, provide guests with the answers. Award the person with the most correct answers a prize.

Guess When the Baby Will Be Born

Print out a monthly calendar of the three months surrounding the mom's due date. Pass the calendar around, and ask guests to write their name on the date they think the baby will be born. If more than one guest has the same date, add approximate time of birth to the note.

When the baby is born, provide an update and a prize for the winner.

TIP: This game works best when played before the baby has been born.

Who's Crowning?

While most baby shower games are naturally sweet and inoffensive, some people might try to take the occasion to a whole new level of questionable taste. Michael seemed to think that a practice run of the birth is a great way to make sure that a father is prepared for the big day. He and Dwight had a lot of fun simulating the birthing process using a watermelon. If you feel like doing the same, you could ask for volunteers to line up in front of the expecting couple, and have them share their best "crowning" impressions, one at a time. Ask guests to vote on who birthed the baby the best. And then never speak of it again.

TIP: While watermelon births aren't a required part of this game, they can help add realism to the experience. Just be sure not to over-butter your melon unless you want to scar everyone watching, including the parents-to-be, for life.

"Babies are one of my many areas of expertise. Growing up, I performed my own circumcision."

—Dwight Schrute

DÉCOR

Create the perfect backdrop for the shower by decorating with gender-neutral colors. Cream tablecloths and green or yellow streamers are easy additions to bring the party to life.

Place the Scott's Loaded Tater Tots (page 64), Ultra-Feast Macaroni and Cheese (page 66), Watermelon and Feta Salad (page 65), and premixed glasses of The Astird and the Chevy (page 68) together on a table. Drape the Baby Shower Banner (page 70) and Diaper Banner (page 71) near the food and gift displays, and use the Guess the Baby (opposite page) game as a tabletop decoration.

Set up the Mom's or Dad's Throne (page 72) in the middle of the room so the parents-to-be can be showered with attention.

Instead of cups, provide each guest with a baby bottle to drink other libations or cocktails from, and see who the real life of the party is!

Dinner Party

"Michael has asked Pam and me to dinner at least nine times. And every time we've been able to get out of it. But I've got to give him credit, he got me. Because I'm starting to suspect that there was no assignment from corporate."

—Jim Halpert

While not all out-of-the-office events fall under the umbrella of your Party Planning Committee's responsibilities, an unofficial function can provide an ideal opportunity to bond, play games, and even do a bit of business. Hosting a dinner party at your personal residence is an ideal way to expand your camaraderie with your colleagues, letting you get to know more about them while enjoying some dinner, dancing, and drinks. Unless, of course, your hosts are locked in a toxic relationship and things rapidly spiral out of control. But I digress.

Depending on the size of your home or condo, it's unlikely you'll be able to invite everyone on staff, so don't be afraid to be selective with your guest list. For instance, to keep things a bit more intimate, you could make the gathering strictly "couples only." However, you do run the risk of making some of your office mates feel left out. So if they do end up at your door with their former babysitter as a plus-one, be kind and let them in on the fun. Because we still have so many questions . . .

Once your guests have arrived, it's time to give a quick tour of your home—or *casa* as Michael would call it—before diving into a night filled with good food, awkward party games, and captive sales pitches for your partner's latest business venture. If you manage to make it through the evening without anyone faking an emergency to excuse themselves early, you can chalk your party up as a rousing success!

FUN TIP:
Serve dinner at an appropriate time. Unless you're in Spain, where I've heard they often don't even start eating until midnight . . .

Osso Buco

What better way to impress your coworkers than by cooking up a classic Italian meal from scratch? But be prepared: These tender braised veal shanks take time to cook. Lots of time. So if you don't want your risotto to get cold and your party guests to have to fill many uncomfortable hours, make sure to start cooking this dish way in advance.

Prep Time: 15 minutes
Cook Time: 2 hours
Yield: 4 servings

FOR THE OSSO BUCO:

4 medium-size cuts of veal shank, about 3 pounds
Salt and black pepper, to taste
¼ cup all-purpose flour
¼ cup salted butter
4 cloves garlic, minced
1 large yellow onion, chopped
1 large carrot, chopped
2 stalks celery, chopped
1 teaspoon dried oregano
1 bay leaf
1 cup dry white wine, such as Pinot Grigio
One 14-ounce can diced San Marzano tomatoes
2 tablespoons tomato paste
1 cup beef stock

FOR THE GREMOLATA:

½ cup fresh Italian parsley
1 clove garlic
2 teaspoons grated lemon zest

1. Let the veal shanks come to room temperature, and then season each piece with salt and pepper and dust each piece lightly with flour. In a large Dutch oven over medium-high heat, melt the butter, and then add the veal. Cook until the veal is browned on all sides, about 6 minutes. Remove the veal, and set aside.

2. To the same pan, add the garlic and onion. Cook until the onion is translucent and starting to brown, about 8 minutes. Add the carrots, celery, oregano, bay leaf, and wine, and then add the veal shanks back to the pan. Let simmer for 10 minutes.

3. Add the tomatoes, tomato paste, and beef stock, and then season with salt and pepper. Simmer over low heat for about 1½ hours, basting every 15 minutes, until the veal is tender but not completely falling off the bone. If the liquid goes below halfway up the shanks, add more stock and wine.

4. Prepare the gremolata. Add the parsley, garlic, and lemon zest to a food processor, and pulse until combined. Garnish each veal shank with 1 to 2 tablespoons of gremolata before serving.

NOTE: Osso buco can be prepared a day in advance and tastes even better if it sits overnight, covered, in the refrigerator. If you're cooking in advance, reheat the osso buco over medium-low heat, and wait to prepare the gremolata until just before you're ready to eat.

"I don't care what they say about me. I just want to eat. Which I realize is a lot to ask for. At a dinner party."

—Pam Beesly

Roasted Vegetable Risotto

This risotto dish is delicious and can be served as its own meal or alongside the Osso Buco. It is recommended you make the Osso Buco in advance, but if you're cooking everything the same day, you can begin cooking this after the Osso Buco has been simmering for about a half hour. To get the same bright yellow color of Jan's risotto, add the saffron threads to your broth.

Prep Time: 10 minutes
Cook Time: 1 hour
Yield: 4 to 6 servings as a side dish

FOR THE ROASTED VEGETABLES:

2 pounds assorted root vegetables, such as carrots, sweet potatoes, parsnips, onions, or beets
¼ cup olive oil
Kosher salt and black pepper, to taste

FOR THE RISOTTO:

4 to 6 cups chicken or vegetable broth
1 teaspoon saffron threads (optional)
2 tablespoons olive oil
4 cloves garlic, minced
1 medium yellow onion, minced
1 cup arborio rice
1 cup Parmesan cheese
Salt and black pepper, to taste

1. Prepare the roasted vegetables. Preheat the oven to 425°F. Wash the vegetables to remove any excess dirt. For vegetables with edible skins, like carrots and sweet potatoes, leave the skins on. For vegetables with inedible skins, like onions, peel them.

2. Chop the vegetables into bite-size chunks, discarding any roots and stems. In a medium bowl, toss the vegetable pieces with the olive oil, and season with salt and pepper.

3. Spread out the vegetables on a baking sheet. Bake for 25 to 30 minutes, until browned and fork-tender. Set aside, and tent loosely with foil to keep them warm.

4. While the vegetables are cooking, prepare the risotto. Add the chicken or vegetable broth into a pot over medium heat to warm. If using saffron, add the threads to the broth now.

5. In a large skillet over medium-high heat, heat the olive oil, and then add the garlic and onion. Cook, stirring often, until the onion is starting to turn translucent, 6 to 8 minutes. Add the rice, and cook for another 2 to 3 minutes. You want the rice to toast slightly before you add any liquids.

6. Reduce the heat to medium. Add about 1 cup of the warm broth, and stir the mixture until the liquid is absorbed. This will take about 3 to 5 minutes. It's important to be patient and allow the liquid to fully absorb before adding more. Repeat until you've added at least 4 total cups of liquid. You'll know the risotto has enough liquid when it's no longer absorbing more, and there is no firmness left to the grains when you taste test them. As you get closer to the end, add the liquid in smaller increments so you don't accidentally end up with watery risotto.

7. Remove the pan from the heat, and stir in the cheese until melted. Season to taste with salt and pepper. To serve, place the risotto in a serving dish, and top with the roasted vegetables. Serve immediately. Risotto will get gummy as it sits or when it's reheated.

"I hope she didn't do anything to the food. I can't prove it . . . but I think she might be trying to poison me."

—Michael Scott

Beet Salad

This rustic beet salad is a great side dish to bring to any dinner party (even the ones where you weren't asked to bring any food). The earthy flavors pair well with just about everything, from Osso Buco to random cold turkey legs. While this salad looks lovely plated and served, it's honestly just as tasty when eaten straight from the plastic container.

Prep Time: 15 minutes
Cook Time: 1 hour
Yield: 4 servings

2 pounds beets
1 lemon
6 ounces fresh chèvre
Kosher salt and black pepper, to taste
1 bunch watercress, chopped and with roots removed
½ cup chopped fresh dill

1. Clean the beets, and remove the stems. In a large saucepan over high heat, bring a pot of water to a boil. Add the beets, and boil for 45 minutes to 1 hour, until fork-tender. Remove from the water, and set aside to cool.

2. While the beets are cooking, prepare your dressing. Zest the lemon rind into small pieces using a zester, or peel the yellow rind off with a peeler and finely chop it. In a large glass bowl, add the chèvre and lemon zest, and then juice the lemon into the bowl. Add salt and pepper, and then whip the mixture together using a hand mixer until all ingredients are combined and the cheese has become soft and airy.

3. When the beets are cool, peel them. If the beets are cooked enough, the skin should slide off easily with your hands and a paper towel. Chop them into bite-size pieces.

4. Add the beets, watercress, and dill to the dressing bowl, and stir well to combine. Serve chilled.

"We came here to eat dinner and to party. This is a dinner party, right?"
—Dwight Schrute

Bold Red Sangria

When throwing a dinner party, a bottle of wine is a customary hosting gift. Of course, no matter how hard you try, there's a chance that your host will only deem your contribution worthy of cooking with. If you want a drink everyone is sure to enjoy, then try making a batch of this fruity sangria. It really doesn't matter what kind of wine you use. Michael used one with an "oaky afterbirth." (If you don't have enough wineglasses for everyone, make sure to have guests bring their own!)

Try to make the sangria the night before. The longer it sits, the better the flavor will be.

Prep Time: 10 minutes
Yield: 8 servings

2 apples, thinly sliced
1 orange, thinly sliced
1 lemon, thinly sliced
1 cup pomegranate juice
1 cup brandy
½ cup orange liqueur
2 bottles bold red wine, such as Malbec

1. Combine the fruit in a pitcher, and pour the liquids in on top.

2. Allow to rest, covered, overnight in the refrigerator (or at least a few hours).

3. Serve in large wineglasses or highball glasses, over ice, making sure to include some fruit pieces in each glass.

NOTE: Feel free to get creative with the fruit—try adding dark berries, maraschino cherries, or other citrus—and the juices you add. If you like a lighter sangria, top each glass with sparkling water as you serve it.

"Nothing disturbing here. Just a couple of friends having an awesome dinner party."
—Michael Scott

CRAFTS

Serenity by Jan Candles

Although "serenity" seems to be the opposite of what Michael and Jan's infamous dinner party inspired, I'll admit that the smell of these homemade candles did help to soothe the trauma left from that evening. You can light these candles to create ambience at your own dinner party—as long as you promise not to use them to convince your guests to invest in your candle-making endeavors.

Use heat-safe jars that are relatively thick for safety, and be sure to buy candlewicks that are taller than your glass jars. Serenity by Jan labels can be downloaded from the online resources page if you want to relive that moment for some strange reason.

SUPPLIES

- **Microwavable soy wax**
- **Essential oils**
- **Candlewicks with metal bases**
- **Heat-safe jars**
- **Computer**
- **Printer**
- ⬇ **Serenity by Jan Label Template**
- **Printer labels**

1. Heat the soy wax in a microwave-safe container. Once fully melted, add 5 to 10 drops of essential oil to the wax, and stir. Use more or less oil to obtain the scent you wish to create.

2. Dip the bottom of the candlewick in the melted wax. This will help the wick stay in place. Place the candlewick in the center of the heat-safe jar. If you have a very long wick, you can tie the wick to a pencil or skewer to hold it in place while the wax sets. You can also use a long clip or wick holder.

3. Pour the melted wax into the jar, being careful to keep the wick in place. Make sure the wick is still centered. Allow to set.

4. Using a computer and printer, create and print "Serenity by Jan" labels.

5. Label each jar accordingly.

"Did you know that candles are the number-one fastest-growing product in the scent aroma market? Two-billion-dollar-a-year industry."

—Michael Scott

One Night Place Settings

Choosing the right music for your dinner party can ease the mood and pass the time while you wait for your Osso Buco to finish cooking. Choosing the wrong music can leave everyone uncomfortable and eager to find excuses to leave. Or worse. Fortunately, even the worst CDs can be put to good use as place settings. You won't be able to listen to these CDs afterward, but you'll never forget the music—but to be fair, that's probably for the best.

SUPPLIES
- **12 old CDs per place setting**
- **Hot-glue gun**

1. Arrange the CDs in a grid, four across and three down. Align them so the "sides" are overlapping by about a centimeter or so.

2. Use hot glue to glue the CDs together between the overlaps. Let the glue dry.

3. Display shiny side up.

TIP: While you wait for dinner to be ready, pick an uncomfortable song to listen to on repeat while you dance. The more you get into the music, the better.

"THAT ONE NIGHT"

BY HUNTER RAYMOND

You took me by the hand.

Made me a man.

That one night. (One night.)

You made everything all right.

So raw, so right.

All night, all right.

Oh yeah, Oh yeah.

Wineglass Charms

When you've got a limited number of wineglasses at your disposal, it's extremely important that everyone keep track of their glass. Wineglass charms make it easy for everyone at the party to identify their glass, no matter how many times it's been refilled. Be sure to make a few extra, just in case more guests show up with glasses of their own!

SUPPLIES

- **Jewelery pliers**
- **Large hoop earring wires**
- **Glass beads in a variety of colors**

1. Use the jewelry pliers to open the end of the earrings so there is a small gap between the loop and the hook of the earring wire. Do not open the wires too wide, or they will lose their shape.

2. String beads onto the wire into decorative patterns. Each charm should have unique patterns or colors. Use the pliers to reshape the wire if necessary, or use your hands to hook the earring wire together so the beads do not fall off.

Dunder Mifflin Charades

The Office spawned many amazing and laugh-out-loud moments during its nine seasons. Relive your favorite memories with a hilarious game of Dunder Mifflin Charades.

Just fill a bowl or hat with scraps of paper listing some of your favorite Dunder Mifflin memories. Feel free to go deep. Nothing is off the table, every moment is in play.

Divide into two teams. The first team selects a piece of paper from a bowl and nominates a player to act out the clues. Set a timer for one minute.

Without using words, the player must act out the clues while their teammates guess. Correctly guessed answers earn that team points. When time runs out or the answer is guessed, the turn changes to the other team.

SOME SUGGESTIONS TO GET THE IDEAS FLOWING

- **Kevin bringing his chili to the office**
- **Dwight's infamous fire walk**
- **Michael's grilled foot injury**
- **Andy's unfortunate dance injury**
- **Jim and Pam's flash-mob wedding**
- **Dwight gets a pumpkin stuck on his head**
- **Meredith's hair catches fire**

"Michael and Jan seem to be playing their own separate game. And it's called 'Let's see how uncomfortable we can make our guests.' And they're both winning."

—Jim Halpert

Investment Opportunity

Nothing says "fun" like forcing your guests to enter into an awkward business relationship. In loving memory of Serenity by Jan, make everyone pitch their worst company idea. Give everyone an 8½-by-11-inch piece of paper to create a promotional poster, and let them present their business concept. Attendees can then vote on which company they would be most likely to invest in, as well as which one is the absolute worst idea. Sure, we all know candles are the number-one fastest-growing product in the scent aroma market, but if you're lucky, your idea might end up being the next big hit. But probably not.

DÉCOR

A dinner party is the ideal way to get to know coworkers outside of the office. Invite a variety of coworkers to liven up the conversation and to allow guests to mingle with people they might not have the opportunity to connect with every day.

Select a classic theme for the evening using a warm color scheme and simple tablecloths. Set the table with your finest matching dishware and utensil sets—and One Night Place Settings (page 85) if you've got them. And of course, don't forget to tidy up—even if you can't do anything about the cracked window or beer sign hanging nearby. Assemble a centerpiece for your table by placing your DIY Dundies (page 33) in the middle of the table, and light a few Serenity by Jan Candles (page 84).

If you are cooking before your guests arrive, your home will be filled with the aroma of the delicious Osso Buco (page 78) and Roasted Vegetable Risotto (page 80) you've made. If you're starting the food right when they get there like Jan did, well, don't worry, the aromas will catch up!

Set out a few appetizers for people to snack on before dinner, such as a bowl of maraschino cherries and a bowl of olives. When your guests arrive, pour a few glasses of Bold Red Sangria (page 83) and hand out Wineglass Charms (opposite page) for your guests to keep track of their drinks.

Finer Things Club

in progress,
please be respectful.

A ROOM
WITH A VIEW

Finer Things Club Meeting

"Oscar, Toby, and I are founding members of the Finer Things Club. We meet once a month to discuss books and art, celebrate culture in a very civilized way. Sometimes the debate can get heated, but we're always respectful. There is no paper, no plastic, and no work talk allowed. It's very exclusive."

—Pam Beesly

Has the modern workplace begun to feel a bit too mundane? Would it help you to return to another age? A time of refinement and civility? Then starting a new chapter of the Finer Things Club might be the perfect escape for you. Devoted to the pursuit of enlightenment, this legendary, exclusive organization is for anyone who gazed out at an ocean of gray cubicles and found only ennui.

Oscar, Toby, and Pam started the Finer Things Club as a rare opportunity to celebrate sophisticated culture in a civilized way. From reading Edwardian novels while sipping tea from fine china to admiring Impressionist art while eating berries and wearing berets, their meetings made the time go by quicker and the boredom of the office significantly more tolerable. Now, using their original club as a template, you too can experience that same *joie de vivre*.

Some lessons from the show:

Firstly, keep the member list small, as every time the club tried to add a new member, it didn't work out quite as well as they would have liked.

Secondly, since a club of such high prestige is naturally focused on uncommon delights, it goes against its very nature to hold meetings in the office's common areas. Examinations of such cultural significance should never be muddled by the beeping of a microwave, the jingle of coins in a vending machine, or the unsolicited opinions of a nosy nonmember. So find a cozy, undisturbed corner of the office, and prepare to explore the finer things in life.

FUN TIP:

Stick to the rules! Members of your chapter of the Finer Things Club should work together to set some basic expectations to help meetings run smoothly. For instance, the original chapter had a different theme for each meeting that inspired their choices in food, attire, and reading material. You don't have to follow their lead, but whatever you decide to do, just make sure you're all on the same page.

Finger Sandwiches Two Ways

With two unique preparations on the menu, these delicate canapés are paired perfectly with hot tea and stimulating conversation. Whether you prefer cucumber and herb or truffled deviled egg, these finger sandwiches are, as Finer Things Club nonmember Andy once said, "finger-lickin' delicious."

CUCUMBER AND HERB

Prep Time: 10 minutes
Yield: 15 finger sandwiches

4 ounces cream cheese, room temperature
¼ teaspoon garlic powder
¼ teaspoon onion powder
2 teaspoons assorted dried herbs, such as dill, parsley, or thyme, or 2 tablespoons chopped fresh herbs
1 English cucumber, cut into 15 ⅛-inch-thick slices
1 baguette, cut into 15 ¼-inch-thick slices
Pink Himalayan sea salt, for garnish

1. In a medium bowl, combine the cream cheese with the garlic powder, onion powder, and herbs. Refrigerate for at least 30 minutes or overnight to allow flavors to deepen, and then adjust to taste.

2. Assemble the sandwiches by spreading about 1 tablespoon of the cream cheese on one flat side of each slice of bread, top with a slice of cucumber, and garnish with a sprinkle of sea salt if desired. Serve open-faced.

TRUFFLED EGG SALAD

Prep Time: 15 minutes
Cook Time: 15 minutes
Yield: 10 finger sandwiches

8 eggs
¼ cup mayonnaise
2 teaspoons Dijon mustard
2 tablespoons minced chives, plus more for garnish
1 teaspoon white truffle oil
½ teaspoon kosher salt
⅛ teaspoon ground black pepper
1 baguette, sliced into 10 ¼-inch-thick rounds

1. First, boil the eggs: Place eggs in a medium saucepan, and fill with water so that the eggs are totally submerged by at least an inch of water. Bring the water to boil over high heat. Allow the eggs to boil for 60 seconds, and then turn off the burner, cover the pan, and allow to sit for 10 to 12 minutes. Remove the eggs from the water, and immediately place into a bowl of ice water to stop cooking. Once eggs are cool, peel and discard shells.

2. Place the eggs in a medium bowl, and mash with a fork until you have a chunky consistency.

3. Gently mix in the mayonnaise, mustard, chives, truffle oil, salt, and pepper. If you prepare the egg salad in advance and refrigerate it, the truffle flavor will deepen significantly, so be careful of adding more to taste until just before you serve.

4. Assemble the sandwiches by spooning about a tablespoon of egg salad onto the flat side of a slice of baguette, garnish with more chives, and serve open-faced.

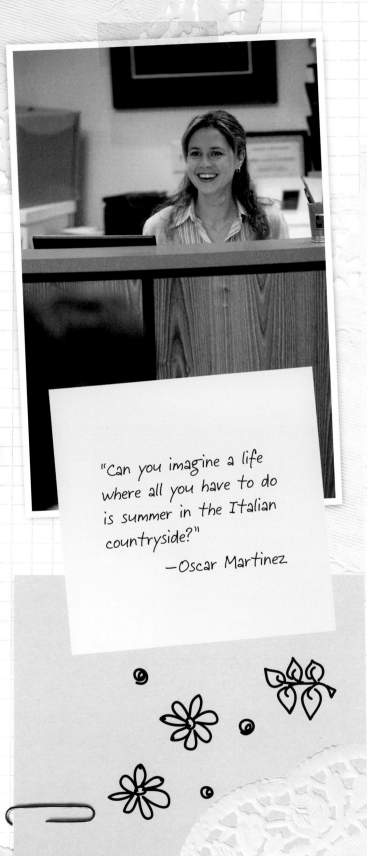

"Can you imagine a life where all you have to do is summer in the Italian countryside?"

—Oscar Martinez

Lemon Tea Cookies

These delightful tea cookies pair perfectly with tea or an Earl Grey Cocktail (page 92).

Prep Time: 1 hour 15 minutes (including chilling time)
Cook Time: 10 minutes
Yield: 24 cookies

3 cups all-purpose flour
1 teaspoon baking powder
½ teaspoon salt
1¼ cups (2 sticks plus 2 tablespoons) unsalted butter, softened
1 cup granulated sugar
¾ cup confectioners' sugar, divided
2 eggs
Juice of ½ a lemon
2 teaspoons grated lemon zest

1. In a medium mixing bowl, combine the flour, baking powder, and salt. In a large mixing bowl, cream the butter, granulated sugar, and ½ cup confectioners' sugar until light and fluffy. Add the eggs, lemon juice, and lemon zest, and stir to combine.

2. Add the flour mixture to the wet mixture in thirds, mixing well after each addition. Cover the bowl, and refrigerate for at least 1 hour.

3. Preheat the oven to 350°F.

4. Using your hands, roll dough into 1-inch balls, working quickly so the dough doesn't become too warm. Place on a lined cookie sheet 3 inches apart, and then use the bottom of a glass to flatten each ball into a ⅛- to ¼-inch-thick disc.

5. Bake until cookies are pale gold, about 10 minutes. Remove from the oven, allow to cool, and dust with the remaining ¼ cup confectioners' sugar. Serve.

Earl Grey Cocktail

Prep Time: 30 minutes, including cooling time
Yield: 2 servings

FOR THE TEA:

2 bags Earl Grey tea
1¼ cups water
1 tablespoon honey

FOR THE COCKTAIL:

1 cup brewed tea
2 ounces gin
1 ounce bergamot liqueur
2 lemon twists, for garnish
2 sprigs lavender, for garnish

1. Prepare the tea. In a medium saucepan over high heat, bring the water to a boil, and then remove from heat. Add the tea bags, and steep for 4 to 5 minutes. Remove the bags, and add the honey while the tea is still hot, stirring to dissolve. Allow to cool.

2. Prepare the cocktails. Fill a shaker with ice, and then add the tea, gin, and bergamot liqueur. Shake until chilled, and pour into two bone china teacups. Garnish with a lemon twist and a sprig of lavender.

NOTE: If you cannot find bergamot liqueur, use 3 ounces of gin instead of 2. You may need to use slightly more honey in the tea.

Butter Shortbread

Fill your Tiered Tray (page 96) with this selection of delectable confections that are sure to sweeten up whatever fun read your book club has selected.

Prep Time: 5 minutes
Cook Time: 40 minutes
Yield: 16 pieces

1 cup (2 sticks) cold unsalted butter
½ cup sugar, plus more for sprinkling
½ teaspoon salt
2 cups all-purpose flour

1. Preheat the oven to 325°F.

2. Line an 8-by-10-inch baking pan with parchment paper, allowing a few inches to hang over the edges. You can grease the bottom and sides of the pan with some butter to help the parchment paper stick to the pan and make it easier to work with.

3. Cut the butter into ½-inch chunks, and place in the bowl of a stand mixer fitted with a flat beater. Add the sugar and salt, then mix on medium until the mixture looks like small pebbles, about 3 minutes.

4. While the mixer is running, slowly add the flour over the course of 2 minutes. The mixture will look like sand after all the flour has been added.

5. Pour the mixture into the pan, and firmly press the dough flat. Sprinkle with additional sugar.

6. Bake until the shortbread is pale gold, about 40 minutes.

7. Let cool for 10 minutes, then score the top of the shortbread into the cookie shape you'd like (rectangles are an easy option). Allow the shortbread to cool completely, and then remove it using the parchment paper. Cut along the scored lines, and serve.

CRAFTS

Finer Things Club Sign

The most important part of the Finer Things Club is making sure everyone who isn't invited knows they shouldn't interrupt the club. This "Do Not Disturb" sign sends the perfect message, nice and clear.

SUPPLIES

- **Precut wooden plaque**
- **Acrylic paint**
- **Paint pen(s) and/or stickers**
- **Decoupage glue (optional)**

1. Paint the wooden plaque a solid color on both the front and back—white is a clean color that will allow your message to read clearly, but you can use anything else you'd like.

2. Use fine script handwriting and a permanent pen or letter stickers in a contrasting color to write "Finer Things Club in progress, please be respectful."

3. If you're using stickers, finish the sign by painting over the stickers with a thin layer of decoupage glue to seal the lettering.

4. Display by resting the plaque against a stack of books, or get a simple frame holder.

Finer Bookmarks

Keeping track of what you are reading is an important part of participating in the Finer Things Club. Use your artistic skills to create paper bookmarks inspired by your monthly reading selections, not only to save your place, but also to remind you of key points and themes to discuss during club meetings.

SUPPLIES

- **Computer and word processing software**
- **Cardstock**
- **Scissors**
- **Hole punch**
- **Embroidery thread**
- **Glue stick**

1. In your word processing software, set your page to Landscape mode. Type out your favorite quotes, and center the lettering.

2. Print directly onto colored cardstock.

3. Use a sharp pair of scissors to cut around each quote, rounding the edges. Select one short end of each bookmark to create a hole using the hole punch.

4. Wrap embroidery thread around three fingers approximately 10 times, and then cut the end. Cut a separate piece of thread that is roughly four inches long. Gather the threads around your fingers together, and then string the separate thread beneath the threads in your bundle. Slide the single thread to the top of the bundle, and tie a tight knot with the string. This is the top of the tassel.

5. Measure about a ½ inch from the top of the tassel, and tightly wrap a portion of the thread bundle together with additional thread of the same color. Once the top feels secure and looks the way you'd like it to look, tie off the thread. Using your scissors, cut the bottom loops of the tassels to free them. Carefully trim the bottom so the tassel fringe is even.

6. Tie the top of the tassel to your paper markers using the thread at the top of your tassel.

"We need rock and roll, Pam! Rock and roll!"

—Michael Scott

Paper Doily Flowers

Class up your club even more with a beautiful bouquet that will withstand use through several months of meetings. These blooms will make everyone else jealous of how fancy your gathering is.

SUPPLIES

- **Round doilies with a decorative edge, in a variety of sizes**
- **Hot-glue gun or tape**
- **Floral wire**

1. Fold a single doily in half, and then in half again to create fourths.

2. Unfold the doily so there's only one fold. Using the middle crease as a marker, fold the two opposite corners into the center, toward each other. It will look a little like a four-pointed star. Flatten the fold, leaving a diamond shape.

3. Twist the folded bottom of the doily so the edges turn out like petals. Use hot glue or tape to attach the doily to the floral wire, wrapping the folded edges around the wire as you go.

4. Repeat steps 1 and 2 to fold two more doilies. Shape these two doilies around the base doily, and glue them to the floral wire as well. Spread out these additional doily layers to add volume.

5. Create additional flowers by repeating these steps until you have the number of flowers you wish to use in your centerpiece and display in a vase, or use them to augment an existing floral bouquet.

"Besides having sex with men, I would say the Finer Things Club is the gayest thing about me."

—Oscar Martinez

Tiered Tray

It's an indisputable fact that tea cakes and finger sandwiches taste better when served on a beautiful tiered tray. Show off your club's finest snacks by dining in style with a tiered tray.

SUPPLIES

- **Three glass plates in small, medium, and large sizes**
- **Two short glass candlestick holders**
- **Strong food-safe epoxy glue**

1. Stack the plates in order of size, starting with the largest plate.

2. Add a small amount of epoxy glue to the bottom of one candlestick, and attach it to the center of the large plate. Allow to dry completely.

3. Place glue on the top of the candlestick, and then center the medium-size plate on top. Press firmly, and hold for a few minutes to make sure the plate stays in place. Allow to dry completely

4. Repeat step 3 with the smallest plate. Allow to dry completely before using.

FUNTIVITIES

Selecting a Book

The most important element of the Finer Things Club is selecting the right book to read! The frequency you plan to meet should help determine what kinds of books your group will read. If you wish to meet on a monthly basis, it's best to select books that are slightly shorter in length to help ensure everyone has a chance to complete the reading before your gathering. Quarterly meetings might allow for longer books.

When selecting a book, try to come up with something that will inspire not only your party, but your soul as well. The original club focused on a mix of the classics, Pulitzer Prize winners, and authors of color. Some of their favorite selections included *Angela's Ashes*, *Memoirs of a Geisha*, and *A Room with a View*.

DÉCOR

While the book, the company, and the conversation are the most important parts of a Finer Things Club meeting, you can always go the extra mile to properly set the mood.

Ideally, you should find a separate meeting room or office to have your meeting so you're not interrupted by others wandering through your gathering. If you only have access to the break room, you can still elevate the experience with a few decorative flourishes. Use a simple white tablecloth to cover the table, and then decorate it with your Finer Things Club Sign (page 94) to let everyone know they're not invited to this super-exclusive club meeting.

Create a simple centerpiece using flowers augmented with your Paper Doily Flowers (page 95) and candles, and remember to bring real flatware. (No paper or plastic utensils for the Finer Things Club!) Don't forget to set out your Tiered Tray (opposite page) with a variety of delicious snacks. You can line the savory sandwiches on the lower tiers, and then add one of the desserts at the top. Serve the second dessert on a separate serving dish.

Put on some classical music while you're preparing to get in the mood (we suggest Vivaldi's "Four Seasons"). It will also set the scene for other club members as they arrive.

"The Finer Things Club is the most exclusive club in this office. Naturally, it's where I need to be. The Party Planning Committee is my backup, and Kevin's band is my safety."

—Andy Bernard

Not-So-Fine Things

As much as we'd all like to have our Finer Things Club meetings in a setting of complete refinement, sadly, an office just isn't destined to be that place. You have to come to terms with the fact that you will absolutely be interrupted, both by everyday activities and jealous nonmembers. There's no need to get upset when discussing the finer things, so it's up to you to deal with your coworkers calmly when they are:

- Microwaving lunch
- Getting a snack
- Making coffee
- Singing showtunes
- Knocking loudly and telling the club members they have a phone call
- Setting off fire alarms—ILLEGAL!
- Starting their own club at an adjacent table

Clue ①
our character:
Deb U Taunt
(Bill Bourbon's)
niece

Murder Mystery Party

"August 5, 1955. It's a sad day down here in Savannah. Local magnate Bill Bourbon was killed last night, and y'all have congregated tonight for a meal to celebrate Bill as he passes on to his great reward. But you're not just here to pay your respects. You have to figure out which of y'all is the no-account scoundrel who killed him."

—Belles, Bourbon & Bullets

Games have the power to distract people from stressful situations. Working at a midsize paper company, the employees of Dunder Mifflin had a lot of uncertainty when it came to job security, but they knew sometimes the best way to deal with the harsh realities of the business world is simply to escape them for a while. And I do declare, there is no better game to share among associates than a classic murder mystery, like this one Michael made the office play when Dunder Mifflin was on the verge of bankruptcy!

The game itself is deceptively simple. Each person draws a character card that describes who they are and what their alibi is. Everything else is up to the imagination. Players can really get into the action by using props, recreating crime scenes, and speaking in a wide variety of accents that range from Savannah all the way to the Florida panhandle. And since you already know who the killer was in Belles, Bourbon & Bullets, you can write your own murder mystery to keep things fresh when you find yourselves in a similar time of crisis and desperately need the distraction.

If you have enough time to plan ahead, you can add some regional delicacies to the menu to turn the game into a full-blown event and make it feel even more authentic. (Just be careful that the butler doesn't try to poison anyone!) If all goes according to plan, there will be so much murder and intrigue that your little heart will barely be able to take it . . . and, more importantly, your stressful day at the office will fly right on by! There are bound to be more dark days ahead, but at least we know a way to make them a little brighter.

FUN TIP:

Commit to your character. Sure, it may seem silly at first, but it really does make things more fun for everyone if you're willing to play along. But always try to stay aware of the fine line between the game and the real world. It's easier than you'd imagine to get stuck in character, so be careful! Get in too deep, and one imaginary murder could easily unravel into a four-way standoff that lasts hours past closing time. And when that happens, nobody wins.

MENU

Caleb Crawdad's Shrimp and Grits

This dish is as Southern as they come, just like handsome playboy Caleb Crawdad, one of the star characters in Belles, Bourbon & Bullets: A Murder Mystery Dinner Party Game. Caleb may spoon with a different woman every night to make them feel beautiful, but when it comes to dinner, his real spoon is loyal to just one meal. This one!

Prep Time: 10 minutes
Cook Time: 40 minutes
Yield: 6 servings

FOR THE SHRIMP MIXTURE:

2 pounds raw shrimp, peeled and deveined
Juice of 1 lemon
½ teaspoon cayenne pepper
½ teaspoon salt
1 pound andouille sausage, cut into ¼-inch slices
5 slices bacon, cut into 1-inch pieces
1 green bell pepper, chopped
1 red bell pepper, chopped
1 yellow bell pepper, chopped
1 small yellow onion, chopped
4 cloves garlic, minced
¼ cup salted butter
¼ cup all-purpose flour
1 tablespoon Worcestershire sauce
1 cup chicken stock

FOR THE GRITS:

1 cup stone-ground grits (original, not instant)
1 cup shredded cheddar cheese
3 scallions, white and tender green parts only, sliced into rounds
Salt and black pepper, to taste

1. Marinate the raw shrimp in the lemon juice, cayenne pepper, and salt while preparing the rest of the ingredients.

2. Prepare the grits. In a large saucepan over high heat, bring 4 cups of water to a boil. Add the grits, and reduce heat to a simmer. Cook until all the water is absorbed, about 15 minutes. This can be done while cooking the rest of the recipe. Once the water is fully absorbed, shut off the heat and stir in the cheese, scallions, salt, and pepper.

3. In a large skillet, cook the andouille sausage over medium-high heat until golden brown, about 8 minutes. Remove from the pan, and set aside.

4. In the same pan, cook the bacon over medium-high heat until browned and very crispy, about 6 minutes. Remove from the pan, and set aside.

5. In the same pan, add the bell peppers, onion, and garlic. Cook until softened, about 8 minutes.

6. In a medium saucepan, prepare a roux by melting the butter over medium heat and slowly incorporating the flour. Stir constantly until the mixture turns a deep golden brown, about 10 minutes. Be careful to not burn the roux.

7. Add the roux to the skillet with the vegetables, and add the andouille and bacon back in. Add the shrimp with juices, Worcestershire sauce, and chicken stock. Cook over medium heat until the shrimp are white and cooked through, and the sauce has thickened slightly, about 5 minutes. Remove from the heat, and serve over the grits.

Voodoo Mama Juju's Chicken and Andouille Gumbo

Angela couldn't be more opposite of her in-game persona, Voodoo Mama Juju, the witch doctor of the Savannah swamps. She practically got the vapors when she realized that her character was known for her dalliance with the dark arts! Maybe it would have been easier for her to get into her role if she had cooked up some of this hearty gumbo. Now, this here is some real magic, I do declare.

Prep Time: 15 minutes
Cook Time: 1 hour 15 minutes
Yield: 8 to 10 servings

½ cup (1 stick) salted butter
½ cup all-purpose flour
1 large yellow onion, diced
1 large green bell pepper, diced
2 large stalks celery, diced
4 cloves garlic, minced
12 ounces andouille sausage, sliced thin
One 28-ounce can crushed tomatoes
One 16-ounce package frozen okra, cooked according to package directions
1½ pounds cooked, shredded chicken
1 dried bay leaf
1 teaspoon dried thyme
1 teaspoon dried basil
1 teaspoon smoked paprika
1 teaspoon cayenne pepper
1 teaspoon salt
½ teaspoon black pepper
4 cups chicken stock
2 tablespoons cornstarch or 1 tablespoon gumbo filé
6 cups cooked white rice

1. Make the roux. Add the butter and flour to a large stockpot or Dutch oven. Cook over medium heat, stirring constantly, until the mixture is a rich brown color, about 15 minutes. The continuous stirring will keep the roux from burning. If you burn the roux, start over, as a burned roux will make the gumbo bitter.

2. Add the onion, bell pepper, celery, and garlic to the Dutch oven. Cook, stirring often, until vegetables are tender, about 10 minutes.

3. Add the sausage, and cook, still stirring, another 10 minutes, until the sausage is cooked through.

4. Add the tomatoes, okra, chicken, and herbs and spices. Stir to combine, and cook for another 5 minutes.

5. Add the chicken stock, and simmer for about 30 minutes. Adjust seasonings to taste (but remember that the soup will become spicier the longer it sits). Turn off the heat.

6. If you prefer a thinner gumbo, leave the soup as is. For a traditionally thick gumbo, stir in the gumbo filé, or dissolve the cornstarch in 2 tablespoons of water, add to the soup, and give it a stir.

7. Serve the gumbo over white rice.

NOTE: Gumbo filé is a traditional ingredient in gumbo that comes from the sassafras root. It's mostly used for thickening, though. If you can't find it, you can easily substitute cornstarch dissolved in water as a thickening agent. Once you've added filé or cornstarch, do not return the soup to a boil or it will become too thick. Reheat it gently on the stovetop. Gumbo is even better the next day.

Beatrix Bourbon's Pecan Bars

According to the CD included with the game, Beatrix Bourbon was willing to kill for a chance at her family's fortune. Too bad she didn't realize she could have made a killing by selling her signature pecan bars instead. These deliciously decadent desserts are the embodiment of Savannah itself—like molasses, just sort of spillin' out of your mouth!

Prep Time: 10 minutes
Cook Time: 50 minutes
Yield: 24 bars

FOR THE SHORTBREAD CRUST:

½ cup (1 stick) salted butter, cold and cut into chunks
1 cup all-purpose flour
½ cup sugar
Nonstick cooking spray

FOR THE FILLING:

2 eggs, beaten
1 cup sugar
¼ cup light corn syrup
¼ cup dark corn syrup
3 tablespoons salted butter, melted
2 tablespoons good bourbon
2 cups pecan halves, chopped

1. Prepare the shortbread crust. Preheat the oven to 400°F. In a food processor, pulse together the crust ingredients until they're a crumbly mix. Mix together the ingredients, and then press into an even layer in a 9-by-13-inch baking dish greased with cooking spray. Bake for 15 to 18 minutes, until golden brown. Remove from oven.

2. Prepare the filling. Lower the oven to 350°F. Mix together all the ingredients in a medium bowl, and pour over the shortbread. Bake 30 to 35 minutes, until set. Remove from the oven, and let cool completely before cutting into bars.

"It's never the person you most suspect. It's also never the person you least suspect, since anyone with half a brain would suspect them the most."

—Dwight Schrute

Naughty Nelly's Mint Julep

This refreshing Southern libation is one you won't be able to say no to, which is likely why it's named after a vivacious young socialite with a penchant for scandal and a tendency to entertain any offer of romance. One too many of these, sugar, and you're sure to be making out by the horses in no time. (Two too many, and it might be with your brother.)

Prep Time: 5 minutes
Yield: 1 serving

Crushed ice
2 sprigs mint leaves, divided
2 ounces bourbon
1 ounce simple syrup

1. Fill a copper julep cup ⅔ full with crushed ice. If you don't have a julep cup, an old-fashioned glass will work as well.

2. Crush the leaves from 1 sprig of mint, and add to the mug.

3. Top with liquids, and then fill the glass to the top with crushed ice and garnish with the other sprig of mint.

4. Allow the mug to frost for a few minutes, and serve.

"Ooh, doggy! We got a party now!"

—Michael Scott

CRAFTS

A night of murder and mayhem doesn't happen without some meticulous planning. And since you've already solved the game once, you'll need to work up your own new version. Before the game can start, clues and character cards need to be made. While it seems easiest to stick with the existing characters from Belles, Bourbon & Bullets, you could also use the same format to come up with a brand new theme to add some variety.

Party Clues

The key to a murder mystery is keeping the clues and identities secret. Hide your identities and clues in these clue bags until they are ready to be revealed to the guests.

- **10 index cards per person**
- **10 envelopes per person**
- **Cardstock**
- **White paper bags large enough to hold the envelopes**
- **Baker's twine**
- **Hole punch**
- **Pen**

1. Create the characters for your game. You can come up with your own characters, or base some characters on the ones from Belles, Bourbon & Bullets:

   - **Voodoo Mama Juju**
   - **Beatrix Bourbon (the one Dwight "medium suspects")**
   - **Nathaniel Nutmeg**
   - **Naughty Nellie Nutmeg (her boudoir is always open)**
   - **Deb U. Taunt (Bill Bourbon's niece, she would never hurt him!)**
   - **The Butler**
   - **Caleb Crawdad**
   - **The Accountant ("We're havin' problems payin' the people who give us the seeds and the dirt. . . .")**

2. Create 9 clues and a set of 9 dialogue lines for each guest that correspond to their characters and the clue. The tenth envelope should be filled with "solution" cards that indicate how the person was actually involved in the murder, and one single card will reveal the murderer.

TIP: Not feeling up to writing an entire script? Search for prewritten murder mysteries online. No one will ever know you didn't write them yourself, and your secret is safe with me. (Or is it?)

3. Cut tags out of the cardstock, and label them with each of the character's names.

4. Fold each bag over, and use the hole punch to create two holes in the top of the bag.

5. String the twine through the holes, and tie one numbered tag on each bag.

Mug Shot Photo Prop

No one wants to admit that they murdered Bill Bourbon in cold blood, but someone has to be responsible for his death. Part of the fun is figuring out whether it was the Butler or Bill's loving wife, Beatrix Bourbon. To up the suspense, capture everyone's in-character mug shots using these photo props while you try to decipher who might be the killer among you.

- **White paint pen**
- **Ruler**
- **Black cardstock**
- **White stickers in several sizes**

1. Use a white paint pen and a ruler to create 4 divider lines spaced 2 inches apart that run across the cardstock to create three sections for text.

2. Add the words "Scranton Police Department" to the top section and numbers to the bottom.

3. Personalize the sign in the middle with a variety of nefarious deeds if you wish to have a custom option for every guest, or create one generic sign that reads, "Murder."

TIP: If you have access to a letter board, use that instead of crafting a sign. Letter boards are the perfect way to personalize the crime for each guest!

SCRANTON POLICE DEPARTMENT

CRIME: MURDER

0000000432448

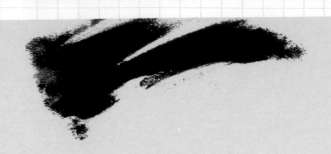

Character Props

Themed props always go the extra mile to help bring your characters to life. Since Belles, Bourbon & Bullets is set in the early 1900s, ladies in attendance can create period-appropriate accessories, like a fan or a fake cigarette holder, to add a bit of authenticity to their character's personality.

FEATHER FAN

- **Wooden craft sticks**
- **Feathers**
- **Hot-glue gun**
- **Black felt**

1. Lay the craft sticks out flat in front of you. Use hot glue to attach feathers to the top portion of the sticks. Set the feathers so they cover the top ¾ of the craft sticks. Let dry.

2. Lay out the sticks in a half circle, with the bottoms stacked so that they overlap on the bottom and create a semicircle on top in a traditional fan pattern. Use hot glue to attach the bottoms of the sticks together. Let dry.

3. Turn over the fan so the feathers are facing the table. Cut the black felt in a half circle that is the same shape and size as the fan. Glue the felt to the fan, and let dry.

FAKE CIGARETTE HOLDER

- **¼-inch diameter wooden craft dowels, at least 12 inches long**
- **Black acrylic paint**
- **White paper**
- **Silver ribbon**
- **Hot-glue gun**
- **Red marker**

1. Paint all but 2½ inches of the dowel black. If the dowel you've purchased is long, carefully cut it down to your desired length.

2. Cut the white paper into a 2½-inch rectangle, and glue it to the unpainted end to create the cigarette.

3. Wrap the silver ribbon around where the paper meets the painted section, and attach with hot glue. Use an opaque ribbon for a better effect.

4. Color the end of the paper and dowel with red marker to give a lit appearance.

"You don't have to keep saying, 'I do declare.' Anytime you say something it means you're declaring."

—Ryan Howard

FUNTIVITIES

Host a Murder Mystery

Michael didn't give the office any advance warning before their Murder Mystery Party, but you're going to want to give your guests proper time to prepare. Prior to the event, provide each guest with an envelope that details their Belles, Bourbon & Bullets character with a motive for why they might have committed the murder. Ask each attendee to dress in the style of their assigned character, and bring along any props that will make their character more believable. You can also make some props for them—like the Fake Cigarette Holder (page 106) or Feather Fan (page 106)—to round out their looks.

When guests arrive, provide each of them with Party Clues (page 105). To begin the game, open the envelope marked "1," and have the guests mingle in character. After a set period of time, have the guests open the second envelope and read the next clue and dialogue line. As each clue is revealed, the guests should act out their lines in character. Halfway through the clues, break for dinner. After dinner, continue the game by opening the next sequential envelope. At the end of the night, have everyone vote on who they think the murderer is, and then everyone should open clue 10—the final envelope—which will reveal who was responsible for the murder.

"Y'all . . ."
—Kevin Malone

"Big-picture stuff. It's about murder."
—Michael Scott

Tips For Writing a New Murder Mystery:

- When creating a murder mystery game, decide how the murderer is chosen and whether or not they know they are the murderer from the beginning. This can be arranged when you send out the character envelopes before the party, or if it is only revealed when the final clue is opened, from the Party Clues (page 105).

- Determine whether or not players (including the murderer) are allowed to lie or only misdirect during gameplay.

- When developing your clues and dialogue lines, provide red herrings and plenty of motives for each character that shine the spotlight on all of the characters throughout the game. Keep everyone guessing until the final clues are read!

> "A lot of the evidence seemed to be based on puns."
>
> —Dwight Schrute

DÉCOR

Belles, Bourbon & Bullets takes place in Savannah, Georgia, and your party should be decorated to set the stage for an evening of Southern mystery. Designate one room as the main game room, and decorate it with florals, soft colors, and creams alongside black highlights to make the ideal backdrop for an evening of intrigue.

Before the guests arrive, set out the Party Clues (page 105) on a table with additional decorations, such as lace or candles. If you made or purchased additional props for your guests to use, lay them around the bags. You can set up a photo booth in a corner of the room by hanging a background against a wall and then placing a camera or a tablet computer on a stand. Set up a table nearby with the Mug Shot Photo Prop (page 105) and any additional character props to allow your guests to take fun and creative photos in character.

You can make drinks to order when the guests arrive, or you can set out a pitcher of Naughty Nelly's Mint Julep (page 104) for guests to serve themselves throughout the evening.

Set the table with a lace runner and fresh flowers. Use milk glasses or other elaborate dishware to complete the look. Serve dinner halfway through the game (around clue four or five), and then finish the evening with Beatrix Bourbon's Pecan Bars (page 103) plus other desserts and libations.

Garden Party

> *"You don't need a reason to throw a garden party any more than you need a reason to throw a birthday party. It's a garden party."*
>
> —Andy Bernard

Certain celebrations demand a level of prestige that an office setting simply won't allow. Whether you're celebrating a promotion or simply trying to prove your worth to your family, a traditional garden party offers a sophisticated escape from the lackluster landscape of the workplace. A garden party is better than any basic picnic or barbecue. Why? Because it's dignified, it's quieter, and there are rules.

Etiquette is of utmost importance at a high-end event like this, so no burping, no slurping, and when eating, take small bites and chew thoroughly with your mouth closed. Keep your elbows off the table, and always remember to dress Connecticut Casual (not to be confused with Pennsylvania Business). This may finally be your excuse to don your favorite scarf, ornamental hat, or expensive toupée.

If you need to brush up on the ins and outs of hosting, *The Ultimate Guide to Throwing a Garden Party*, by the legendary James Trickington, contains all you need to know about announcing your guests, the tableau vivant, and your duties as the party's dance master. Be sure to pay special attention to the section on the evening's mandatory closing ceremonies, particularly when it comes to fire safety.

FUN TIP:

The Garden Party at Schrute Farms went surprisingly well (for everyone except Andy). Consider another agritourism destination for your big bash. Just make sure the farmer's cousin doesn't valet the cars.

Brie and Caramelized Onion Tartlets

Before dinner is served, it is customary for high-end hors d'oeuvres to be offered to your garden party guests. This tantalizing tartlet is bursting with flavor from the combination of melted Brie and caramelized onions, and it pairs perfectly with a bit of marmalade. (That is, if the pot of marmalade you were promised wasn't gifted to your boss's sister instead.)

Prep Time: 5 minutes
Cook Time: 1 hour
Yield: 15 pieces

2 tablespoons salted butter
3 large yellow onions, thinly sliced
1 tablespoon balsamic vinegar
1 teaspoon fresh thyme, plus more for garnish
Salt and black pepper, to taste
15 premade miniature phyllo tart shells
Fifteen 1-by-¼-inch slices of Brie (about ¼ pound)

1. Preheat the oven to 350°F.

2. In a large skillet, melt the butter over medium heat. Add the onions, stirring frequently, until they're a deep golden brown, about 40 minutes. If the onions are starting to burn, reduce the heat slightly, and add a tablespoon or two of water if they're sticking to the pan.

3. Once the onions are caramelized, add the balsamic vinegar and thyme. Season with salt and pepper to taste. Cook another 2 minutes, until everything is fully mixed together.

4. Fill each tart shell two-thirds full with the onion mixture, and top with a piece of cheese.

5. Place the tartlets on a lined baking sheet, and bake until they are golden brown, about 12 minutes. Remove from the oven, garnish with a few more thyme leaves, and serve warm.

NOTE: You can find phyllo tart shells in the freezer section at the grocery store.

Spinach, Bacon, and Blue Cheese Mushroom Caps

A real crowd-pleaser at any festive occasion, these stuffed mushroom caps truly add the "garden" into the garden party. The mix of savory flavors in this recipe work in perfect harmony, like a heartwarming, impromptu father-son duet for your taste buds. It takes *more than words* to explain just how delightful this sumptuous side dish is!

Prep Time: 10 minutes
Cook Time: 25 minutes
Yield: 6 servings as an appetizer

One 16-ounce package cremini mushrooms
Olive oil cooking spray
3 cloves garlic, minced
One 6-ounce package baby spinach, roughly chopped
½ cup blue cheese (or any salty cheese, such as feta, that you prefer)
½ cup bacon pieces, cooked and crumbled
½ cup panko bread crumbs
Black pepper, to taste

1. Preheat the oven to 450°F.

2. Thoroughly clean the mushrooms by wiping them with a damp cloth. Don't rinse them, as that will result in soggy mushrooms. Remove and discard the stems.

3. Place the mushroom caps bottom side down on a baking sheet. Spray lightly with olive oil spray.

4. Cook on the top rack of the oven for about 10 minutes, until mushrooms are browned and tender.

5. Remove from the oven, turn over to release liquid, and set aside. Reduce the oven temperature to 400°F.

6. While the mushrooms are baking, prepare the filling. Lightly coat the inside of a large skillet with cooking spray then heat the pan over medium heat. Add the garlic, and cook for 1 to 2 minutes, until golden. Then, add the spinach and cook until wilted, another 2 to 3 minutes.

7. Turn off the heat, and then stir in the cheese, bacon, and bread crumbs. Season with pepper to taste.

8. On the same baking sheet, fill each mushroom with a heaping spoonful of the filling.

9. Bake just until the cheese is golden brown, about 8 minutes. Remove from the oven and serve.

"Schrute Farms is very easy to find. It's right in the middle of the root-vegetable district. If the soil starts to get acidic, you've probably gone too far."

—Dwight Schrute

Lobster Rolls 2 Ways

Garden parties have sadly earned a reputation for stuffy, outdated cuisine; yet the modern garden party can be about so much more than dry finger sandwiches. Consider exotic meats for your main course to impress your guests. If hippo steaks or giraffe burgers aren't available, then lobster will do just fine. And if you really want to make a splash, why not prepare it more than one way?

"Did I throw this party to impress my parents? That's crazy. Now, if they wanted a garden party, they could throw one themselves. Which, as a matter of fact, they did last week. They threw one for my baby brother. And it was totally amazing, but I couldn't care less."

—Andy Bernard

HOT GARLIC BUTTER LOBSTER ROLLS

Prep Time: 5 minutes
Cook Time: 10 minutes
Yield: 4 servings (or 8 as an appetizer)

4 split-top hot dog buns (or 8 finger sandwich rolls)
½ cup salted butter, divided
2 cloves garlic, minced
1 pound precooked lobster meat, chopped
2 tablespoons Italian parsley, chopped

1. In a large skillet, melt 2 tablespoons of butter over medium-high heat.

2. Spread apart each bun so that the interior is exposed, and place them split-side down in the pan. Toast for one minute on each side, until golden brown. Remove from the pan.

3. In the same pan, add the remaining butter and garlic. Cook for 1 to 2 minutes, until the butter is melted and the garlic is golden.

4. Add the lobster meat, and toss until heated through and coated with the garlic butter.

5. Remove from the heat, and divide evenly among the buns, spooning the remaining butter over the lobster. Garnish with parsley, and serve.

COLD HERB-LEMON LOBSTER ROLLS

Prep Time: 10 minutes
Yield: 4 servings (or 8 as an appetizer)

¼ cup mayonnaise
1 tablespoon lemon juice
1 stalk celery, diced
2 tablespoons chopped fresh herbs (such as tarragon, chives, and thyme)
Salt and black pepper, to taste
1 pound precooked lobster meat, chopped
4 split-top hot dog buns (or 8 finger sandwich rolls)

1. In a medium bowl, mix the mayonnaise, lemon juice, celery, and herbs. Season to taste with salt and pepper.

2. Mix in the lobster, and adjust the herbs and seasonings to your taste.

3. Spoon into the buns and serve.

Stanley's Baklava

Have you been trying to lose weight after an endless parade of decadent desserts at your office's far-too-frequent birthday parties? If you find that your tastes have changed and you don't like cake anymore, then perhaps this flaky pastry might appeal to your newly sophisticated sweet tooth instead. This classic confection is so refined, it makes the sugar in a sheet cake jealous!

Prep Time: 35 minutes
Cook Time: 40 minutes
Yield: 24 pieces

FOR THE BAKLAVA:

2 cups shelled pistachios
½ cup sugar
1 teaspoon ground cinnamon
½ teaspoon ground cloves
1 pound phyllo dough, thawed
1 cup (2 sticks) salted butter, melted

FOR THE SYRUP:

1 cup water
1 cup sugar
½ cup honey
Juice of ½ a lemon
1 cinnamon stick
1 large strip lemon zest
1 large strip orange zest

1. Preheat the oven to 350ºF.

2. Make the baklava. In a food processor, combine the pistachios, sugar, cinnamon, and cloves.

3. Using a pastry brush, lightly coat a 9-by-13-inch pan with melted butter.

4. Roll out the thawed phyllo dough. Lay one layer of phyllo flat in the pan, and brush it lightly with butter. Repeat until there are 10 sheets. It's important to move quickly, so the phyllo doesn't dry out, and to be extremely gentle to avoid tearing the dough as much as possible.

5. Add just over ½ cup filling in a thin layer over the buttered dough.

6. Repeat the phyllo and butter with 5 more layers of dough, then filling, then 5 layers of dough, then filling. Do this until you have 4 layers of 5 sheets each, then end with the remaining filling. Top that with the remaining 10 layers of phyllo, each brushed with butter.

7. Before baking, score the finished baklava into small pieces. Cut five equally spaced lines the long way, then cut diagonally to make diamond shapes.

8. Bake for 40 minutes, until the top is golden brown.

9. While the baklava is baking, prepare the syrup. In a small saucepan over high heat, bring all ingredients to a boil. Cook for 5 minutes, and then set aside to cool. Remove the cinnamon stick and citrus zest strips.

10. Remove the baklava from the oven, and then pour the cooled syrup over the top. Allow to sit for several hours or overnight, at room temperature, before serving.

Farm Boy Swill

If martini bars are too pretentious for your taste and you're looking for something with a bit more rustic flair to serve at your garden party, this earthy beet cocktail made on-site at Schrute Farms might be exactly the beverage for you. Sure, beet farming may be a young man's game, but after a few sips of this pungent pick-me-up, you'll be ready to trade your party dress for some overalls and wishing you could hit the fields. This is one drink that can't be beet . . . but it is!

Prep Time: 5 minutes
Yield: 1 serving

1½ ounces gin
1½ ounces ginger liqueur
½ ounce beet juice
Juice of ½ a lemon
Thyme sprig, for garnish

1. Fill a shaker with ice, and add the liquids.

2. Shake until well chilled, and strain into a martini glass.

3. Garnish with thyme, and serve.

"Toasts are great. I mean, you toast somebody, they toast you back. It just goes round and round. That's my favorite part about toasts. The reciprocity."

—Andy Bernard

CRAFTS

James Trickington's Garden Party Guide

James Trickington's *The Ultimate Guide to Throwing a Garden Party* should be considered among the finest party-planning guides ever written. But even if you can't get your hands on a rare print edition, you can still share some of the guide's most essential tips with your fellow partygoers. Make copies featuring key highlights and pass them out to help set unrealistic expectations and ensure decorum is followed by all attendees.

SUPPLIES

- Computer
- ⬇ *The Ultimate Guide to Throwing a Garden Party* template
- Printer
- White printer paper
- Scissors
- Green wrapping paper or other large sheets of green paper
- Hardback book
- Tape
- Glue stick

1. Download *The Ultimate Guide to Throwing a Garden Party* template from our online resources. Use a printer to print out the labels.

2. Cut out the labels, leaving white space around each.

3. Unroll the wrapping paper so the design is facing down and set the book in the middle. To determine the proper paper size for your book, open the book flat on the paper, and mark so there is at least 1 inch of extra space at the top and bottom of the book, and at least 3 inches extra on both sides. Cut the paper.

4. Return the book to the middle of the paper. Fold the top and bottom of the paper against the edges to fit the paper to the same height as the book. Remove the book, and create a sharp crease along the fold.

5. Close the book, and return to the middle of the paper. Pull the paper around the front and back of the book cover, and fold the overhanging paper over the book's side edges. Create a sharp crease, and then insert the book covers into the flaps you've just created. Tape the cover with a small piece of tape on the top and bottom of the flaps to hold the cover together.

6. Center Label 1 on the top half of the book cover. Affix with a glue stick.

7. Center Label 2 on the bottom half of the book cover. Affix with a glue stick.

8. You can also type and print out each of the chapters for the book and paste them into the first couple of pages of your book with a glue stick.

CHAPTER 1

A proper garden party must be valeted, even if you have to park the automobiles in the hindmost part of your eerie cornfield.

CHAPTER 2

Announcing guests as they enter is the height of decorum and a must. The more volume displayed, the more honor is bestowed upon everyone present.

CHAPTER 3

Respectable dress is "colonial tea party chic," which includes but is not limited to hooped gowns, wigs, and velvet breeches.

CHAPTER 4

One of the host's most important duties is as dance master. A proper courtly dance sets the tone for the entire afternoon.

CHAPTER 5

Certainly do not provide napkins. Mannerly people never spill, and they will be vastly insulted if you imply they possibly could.

CHAPTER 6

Hire a brass band, and have them play time-honored American favorites such as "Hey Mickey," "Macarena," "Peanut Butter Jelly Time," and so forth.

CHAPTER 7

Speak in a British accent. Think Anne Hathaway in that new romantic drama meets Madonna circa 1995. Your guests will be dazzled and intrigued.

"When all this is over, I'd like to actually go to one of Trickington's parties. They sound like a blast."

—Dwight Schrute

CHAPTER 8

The host should present something spectacular to draw the attention of the guests, such as an ice sculpture or a pool filled with Italian wine.

CHAPTER 9

The tableau vivant is not only welcome but expected entertainment at any garden party.

CHAPTER 10

You must perform closing ceremonies that involve carrying lit torches. This will prove your flaming compassion for the perfect garden party.

Sunflower Centerpieces

Borrowing from the beauty of the outdoors, faux sunflowers bring a bright garden atmosphere to the tables at your garden party. If real sunflowers are in season, consider using those instead!

SUPPLIES

- **Scissors**
- **Floral foam**
- **Galvanized bucket**
- **Faux sunflowers and greenery**

1. Cut the floral foam to fit in the base of the bucket.

2. Trim the sunflowers so they appear 6 to 8 inches above the top of the bucket. Insert them into the floral foam. Pay attention to spacing so that the bucket looks full while ensuring flowers are not clustered.

3. Trim the greenery to varying heights, and fill in any areas not covered by sunflowers. Greenery makes the arrangement look complete and does not need to be used sparingly.

Paper Torches

Of all the host's duties at a garden party, none are quite as important as the staging of the closing ceremonies to cap off the festivities. For settings where open flames are not welcome, this paper torch has been officially approved as a substitution by the Trickington Foundation. Probably.

SUPPLIES

- **Brown cardstock**
- **Glue stick**
- **Scissors**
- **Yellow, red, and orange tissue paper**
- **Craft glue**

1. Roll the cardstock into a simple cone, and firmly glue with a glue stick. You may need to use a paper clip to hold the cone closed while it dries.

2. Cut the tissue paper into 6-by-6-inch squares.

3. Bring 1 square each of red, yellow, and orange paper together. Twist the corner. Repeat until you have enough flames to fill the cone.

4. Put a drop of glue on the twisted end, and attach to the inner sides of the cone. Repeat until all flames are attached to the cone, and repeat until you have as many paper torches as needed.

"Can't wait. A folk colonialist gathering when unemployment's at 9%. I wouldn't miss it for the world."

—Ryan Howard

Basil Party Favors

Looking for a perfect party favor for your guests, but you're fresh out of marmalade? A potted basil plant is a great backup option!

SUPPLIES

- **Computer and word processing software or pen**
- **Cardstock**
- **Scissors**
- **Ribbon**
- **Packages of basil seeds**
- **Small terra-cotta pots**
- **Tulle**

1. Create tags using cardstock and scissors. Write or print "From our garden to yours" on the tag.

2. Cut pieces of ribbon around 20 inches long or so, as you will be tying a bow with these ribbons.

3. Place 1 package of seeds in each pot. You should have the same number of seed packages and pots as you will guests.

4. Cut a piece of tulle large enough that you can wrap it around the pot with a few inches extra at the top. Set the pot in the middle of this piece of tulle, and bring the tulle up and around the pot. Center the ribbon around the top of the tulle, using the ribbon to tie a tight knot around the tulle. Slide the tag onto the ribbon, and position the tag next to the knot. Tie the rest of the ribbon into a bow.

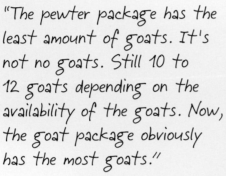

SCRANTON · PENNSYLVANIA
Schrute Farms
BED & BREAKFAST

"The pewter package has the least amount of goats. It's not no goats. Still 10 to 12 goats depending on the availability of the goats. Now, the goat package obviously has the most goats."

—Dwight Schrute

Spontaneous Sing-Along

Just when you thought things couldn't get any more awkward on the show, Andy always found a way of proving they could. Like the time he brought out a guitar in an ill-conceived attempt to impress his guests—and his parents—with his musical talents. If any of your guests try something similar, throw them a bone. When they're done, don't just sit in the awkward silence, start singing your own song so their attempt isn't so out of place and strange.

SONG SUGGESTIONS:

"More Than Words"
"Forever Young"

Raise a Toast

Your garden party may have been thrown to pay tribute to one specific coworker, but once a glass gets raised in their honor, there's no need to end the outpouring of admiration (or the pouring of champagne). Now's the perfect chance for you to say "cheers" to your boss, your unborn child, or even the troops (on both sides). But remember, you can't triple toast somebody until you've hit everyone at least once!

"Get up there and sing or I will cut your larynx and you'll never be able to sing again."

—Meredith Palmer

Garden Party Etiquette

Dwight and Andy—and Mose, as well—took a lot on their shoulders to make their garden party a success. When you plan your own, spread out the responsibilities between a number of committee members. It might help to make copies of *The Ultimate Guide to Throwing a Garden Party* and hand them out, in order to ensure that everyone is properly prepared to do their part.

Encourage all guests to dress in colonial tea party chic. Hoop skirts, wigs, jackets, and breeches are all appropriate attire. If they refuse to dress according to guide standards, make sure they are at least dressed Connecticut Casual or do not permit them entry.

Upon arrival, the last guest to have arrived should valet the car. Is this safe or ideal? No, but it's better than Mose parking it. You will then have to wait for the next guest to arrive, then park their car for them. Only then will you be able to go into the party.

Once inside the party, someone will announce your name at the top of his or her lungs. You should provide them with a list of everyone's names so they don't mistake someone's wife for, well, *someone else*. Then it's your turn to wait to announce the next guest's name.

Dwight performed a memorable dance at his garden party. It certainly set a tone. The guide encourages you to follow suit. Feel free to follow his choreography, or just make up your own. As long as it's elegant, you can't go wrong.

Finally, when the event is over, be sure all your guests leave with their Paper Torch (page 121) and a flourish for the closing ceremonies.

DÉCOR

Since your party is taking place outdoors, the primary atmosphere is set by the garden itself. Ideally, you should select a beautiful corner of your garden, yard, or farm, with enough space to set out plenty of chairs and tables.

Drape the tables with white-and-red-checkered linens, and work to establish a New England look and feel. Place Sunflower Centerpieces (page 121) in the middle of the tables.

Set up a table to the side, and place your copy of James Trickington's Garden Party Guide (page 118) in the center, and then arrange your Basil Party Favors (page 122) and Paper Torches (page 121) in lines on the table.

Arrange the Brie and Caramelized Onion Tartlets (page 112), Spinach, Bacon, and Blue Cheese Mushroom Caps (page 113), Lobster Rolls 2 Ways (page 114), and Stanley's Baklava (page 116) on serving trays, and place them on a table. Arrange additional Sunflower Centerpieces and wicker baskets filled with leafy vegetables (especially beets) to help set the stage.

Prank

Once everyone has safely arrived to the party, sneak to the valet stand and grab all of their car keys and hide them in strategic places throughout the venue. Then, when the time comes to leave, place a forged note allegedly from one of the guests saying that they took the keys. Then sit back and watch as your coworkers, who were already desperate to begin their long drives home, scramble to find a way out.

Beach Games

> *"I have the most boring job in the office, so why wouldn't I have the most boring job on beach day?"*
>
> —Pam Beesly

You know the old saying, "Life's a beach"? Well, since virtually every waking moment of your life is spent at the office, it only seems natural to make work a beach as well. When a party comes along that simply can't be contained within the basic white walls of a conference room, that's when nature calls. So it's time to grab your towel, swimsuit, and book of management parables, and get on board the *par-tay* bus for a trip your office mates will never forget!

While most beach days are a chance to relax and recharge, on the show, Michael turned the trip into a secret battle royale to pick his successor. Things got pretty intense. And in the end, Michael didn't get the job at corporate, so the competition was moot anyway. So if you're looking for some mandatory fun activities—Funtivities—to play at your future beach day inspired by the episode, along with some great food and drinks, this is your section!

While the Kevin of your office might prefer to lie on the beach and eat hot dogs all day, remember this is still a work-sponsored event. These funtivities are all very fun, but if you feel like kicking it up a notch, try sumo wrestling and walking on hot coals. Hopefully with these tips your next beach day will be fun while also being good for team building, testing candidates for promotion, or just proving something to yourself. Let's face it, things will probably get out of hand like they did on the show, but if you follow these tips, everybody will feel like they've won—even if they've lost. Oh, and watch out for snakes!

FUN TIP:

Have fun! While you shouldn't expect any beach days to be nearly as intense as the beach day on the show, you never really know what might happen! Either way, don't lose sight of the fact that you're still getting paid to go to the beach during normal work hours. Enjoy the atmosphere, and use the time between competitions to bond with coworkers who might not normally open up to you in the office. I know the Funtivities can make tempers flare, but if we all try to keep our emotions in check, this could actually be a day worth writing about!

MENU

Hot Dog Bar

Michael seems to think that hot dog eating contests are the pinnacle of human athleticism. But making hot dogs can be just as fun as "sliding them down your gullet," as he so eloquently put it, especially when you've got a variety of next-level ingredients to choose from—including three fresh-made salsas. Hopefully, no one is going to force you to eat fifty-four and a half of these . . . but once you get a taste of one, you'll probably want to try for a new record! After you grill your hot dogs and buns, top them with any of these three sauces.

SPICY AND SWEET RED PEPPER RELISH

Prep Time: 10 minutes
Cook Time: 30 minutes
Yield: about 2 cups

3 to 5 red chile peppers, depending on desired spice level
20 jarred sweet pickled peppers
½ small red onion
1 cup apple cider vinegar
½ cup sugar

1. Wearing plastic gloves, remove the stems and seeds from the red chile peppers. Add to a food processor with the pickled peppers, onion, and pulse until coarsely chopped. You want to retain some texture to the vegetables.

2. Transfer to a medium saucepan, and add the vinegar and sugar. Over medium heat, simmer for 5 minutes, then reduce heat to medium-low and cook for another 20 to 25 minutes, until the mixture has thickened and the flavors have melded. Adjust the flavor to your taste: add sugar for a sweeter relish, or more chile pepper (or red pepper flakes) for more spice. Use as a condiment on hot dogs, sandwiches, or Scrantonicity Sliders (page 46). This will keep in the refrigerator for 1 week.

NOTE: If you can't find jarred sweet pickled peppers, use red bell peppers. You may want to add more chili peppers in that case.

BACON AND CHEESE SAUCE

Cook Time: 10 minutes
Yield: about 2 cups

2 tablespoons salted butter
2 tablespoons all-purpose flour
½ teaspoon garlic powder
1 cup whole milk
1 cup grated yellow cheddar
½ cup grated fontina
6 slices bacon, cooked and crumbled
Salt and pepper, to taste
4 scallions, tender green and white parts only, sliced into rounds

1. In a medium saucepan over medium heat, melt the butter. Whisk in the flour and garlic powder to make a roux. Whisk until completely smooth, about 2 minutes.

2. Slowly add the milk, whisking as you go so the roux incorporates in a totally smooth way. This process should take another 1 to 2 minutes.

3. Add ⅓ of the cheese, and then stir until smooth. Repeat this process until the cheese is fully melted and the sauce is lump-free, 3 to 4 minutes. Add the bacon, and then season to taste with salt and pepper.

4. To serve, pour over a hot dog in a roll (or a baked potato, vegetables, or any other food that would be enhanced by a cheese sauce—so pretty much anything!), and garnish with scallions.

Spicy Pineapple Salsa

Prep Time: 15 minutes
Yields: about 4 cups

1 large pineapple
2 to 3 large jalapeños, depending on desired spice level
1 small habanero pepper (optional, depending on desired spice level)
1 small red onion
1 red or green bell pepper
½ cup chopped cilantro
2 tablespoons fresh grated ginger
Juice of 2 limes

1. Make a pineapple bowl. Stand the pineapple on end, and, with your knife as close as possible to the stem without actually cutting into it, slice off one side making one vertical cut. Make sure the stem stays attached to the larger side. Set the smaller piece aside for another use.

2. Remove the fruit from inside the larger side of the pineapple by scoring a ring about ½-inch in from the rind, then loosen the fruit by making vertical and horizontal cuts across the fruit inside. Remove using a spoon. Discard the hard core, and dice the remaining fruit. You'll have about 2 cups of diced pineapple. Place in a medium glass bowl.

3. Wearing plastic gloves, dice the jalapeños and habanero pepper, if using, discarding the stems and seeds. Add to the same bowl.

4. Peel and dice the onion, discarding the skin. Dice the red pepper, discarding the stem and seeds. Transfer to the bowl then add the cilantro and ginger. Juice the limes into the bowl. Stir to combine, and serve in the pineapple bowl.

"I have never seen that look in a man's eyes ever. I thought that I might die. On Beach Day."

—Jim Halpert

Firewalk Grilled Vegetables

What did Michael say that a great manager needs most of all? Courage. But you'd be surprised how few people are willing to walk across a bed of hot coals to prove whether they're corporate leadership material. When Pam did it, she felt like she proved something to herself and it gave her the chance (and the adrenaline) to say the things she wasn't able to otherwise. Although defeating your fears is great, maybe try defeating your hunger and create lasting memories by eating these delightful grilled veggies. Take it from Dwight. It's better to char them instead of yourself.

Prep Time: 10 minutes
Cook Time: 14 minutes
Yield: 10 servings as a side

3 pounds assorted yellow and green squash
2 large Bermuda onions
1 large head broccoli or cauliflower
¾ cup olive oil
Juice of 1 lemon
1 tablespoon red pepper flakes
Kosher salt and black pepper to taste

1. Slice the squash into rounds (or, for a more decorative presentation, on the diagonal into ovals) about ½-inch thick.

2. Peel the onions, and slice into ½-inch rounds. Some natural separation of rings is fine, but don't separate every ring.

3. Slice the broccoli into spears, preserving some stem with each floret. Slice these ends on the diagonal as well.

4. In a large bowl, whisk together the oil, lemon juice, and seasonings. Toss all the vegetables together with this mixture until they're evenly coated.

5. Transfer the vegetables to a grill basket, and place on the bottom rack of a preheated grill. Cook, tossing often, until the vegetables have started to char around the edges but are still slightly crisp, about 12 to 14 minutes.

"I fully expect to burn my feet and go to the hospital. That's the right spirit when doing a coal walk, right?"

—Pam Beesly

CRAFTS

Beach Day Journal

If your boss is like Michael, he will likely insist that someone takes diligent notes throughout the day, keeping track of everyone's "indefinable" qualities. During a beach day, it is an important job, albeit a boring one. Having a well-decorated notebook might help inspire you to work even harder while everyone else is off enjoying themselves.

SUPPLIES

- **Notebook**
- **Scissors**
- **Scrapbook paper, printed photos, or quotes**
- **Decoupage glue**
- **Paintbrush**

1. Use the cover of your notebook as a template and cut scrapbook paper, photos, and quotes into artistic shapes.

2. Lay the cutouts on top of the notebook cover to be sure everything fits and you like the design.

3. Use a paintbrush to apply a thin layer of decoupage glue to the backside of each element and attach it in its intended place on the cover. Allow to dry.

4. Once the arrangement is set, paint a thin layer of decoupage glue on top of the cover to seal in all the edges. Leave to dry overnight before using.

"It's a good day."
—Pam Beesly

Beach Necklace

If you're going to the beach, it's best to look the part. A colorful beach necklace is an ideal way to capture the spirit of the event.

SUPPLIES

- **Necklace fastener**
- **Jewelry cord**
- **Brown, yellow, green, and red beads (or other colors)**

1. Cut a length of jewelry cord to the length you'd like, and then add at least another 2 inches to allow some slack to help you tie the cord to the additional length. Attach the jewelry cord to one of the necklace fasteners.

2. Thread the beads onto the cord. To create the pattern Michael wears during Dunder Mifflin's beach day, use the following color pattern: 5 brown, 1 green, 1 yellow, 1 red.

3. Continue until the necklace is the appropriate length.

4. Tie off the other side of the necklace fastener.

"I want today to be a beautiful memory that the staff and I share after I have passed on, to New York. And if Toby's a part of it, then it'll suck."

—Michael Scott

Tabletop Tennis Table

Got a score to settle with a coworker? There's no better way to do it than with a raucous game of table tennis. When Jim kept losing to Darryl at table tennis, Pam made this net for him to practice with, away from prying eyes and Kelly's gloating. It's easily transportable and fits a standard banquet table, making it perfect to bring along to your beach party! After the food gets served, everyone else can get served, too!

SUPPLIES

- **2 ½-inch diameter wooden dowels**
- **Fabric**
- **Sewing machine and thread**
- **Rubber clamp**
- **Rubber bands**
- **Table**

1. Cut the wood dowels to 10 inches tall.

2. Measure the width of the table you'd like to use, and add 6 inches. Cut a rectangle of fabric that matches that width and with a length of 12 inches. If you are using a standard banquet table, the measurements will be 36 inches wide by 12 inches long.

3. Turn over the fabric so the design side is facing out, and using your sewing machine, use a running stitch to create 1-inch hems on both long sides.

4. Use a running stitch to create a 1½-inch hem on the short sides.

5. Fold the fabric in half, with the design side facing out. If using a standard banquet table, your rectangle should now be 33 inches wide by 5 inches long.

6. Line up the short-side hems, and carefully use a running stitch to create a new seam on the outside along the short sides of the fabric to join them together.

7. Sew a whip stitch across the bottom of the fabric but leave about 1 inch of space on both sides of the hem open, as this is where your dowels will go.

8. Place the clamps on a table.

9. Using rubber bands, firmly attach the dowels to the clamps. Slide the short sides of the fabric through the holes you've left at the bottom of the fabric over the dowels, and you're ready to play.

"I am okay if I lose every single contest today. Honestly. Because I see these contests as an opportunity for me to demonstrate what a good sport I am."

—Andy Bernard

FUNTIVITIES

Egg-and-Spoon Race

Provide each player with an egg and a spoon. The object of the game is to see who gets to the finish line without dropping the egg. Consider adding layers of difficulty by requiring players to run in a relay, making them keep one arm behind their back, or forcing them to wear a blindfold while you shout directions at them. When putting teams together, try to match people properly. If one of your coworkers is like Andy, who had a hard time keeping cool under pressure, and another is like Kelly, who didn't do well when being yelled at—or being told what to do, in general—be sure to put them on separate teams!

Hot-Dog-Eating Contest

As Michael would say, a good employee should be hungry. Hungry for success. Heat up the grill and start cooking as many hot dogs as you can—but regardless of what he said in the episode, you don't need eight hundred or so to do the trick. That would blow the party's entire budget on hot dogs alone! Provide contestants with water, and set a timer to see how many dogs each competitor can consume. Official hot dog contest rules only count dogs that have been eaten with the bun, and condiments are not required. (Any that come back up don't qualify.)

Campfire Sing-Along

When venturing outside the controlled environment of the office, there's a pretty good chance your event won't go exactly as planned. Follow Michael's lead and try not to "cast a pall" over the fun of the day. Instead, end the festivities with a group sing-along around the campfire before you head back into the real world. Even better, bring along everything you need to make s'mores (all you need is chocolate, graham crackers, and marshmallows. How difficult could that be, right?), and everyone will hopefully be able to put some of the day's less fortunate events behind them. Eventually.

SONG SUGGESTIONS
- **"The Gambler"**
- *The Flintstones* **theme song**
- **"Banana Boat Song (Day O)"**
- **"The Lion Sleeps Tonight"**

"I would rather work for an upturned broom with a bucket for a head than work for somebody else in this office besides myself. Game on."
—Stanley Hudson

DÉCOR

It goes without saying that the best backdrop for a beach party is the beach itself! Since the ocean was obviously a bit too far away for a day trip, the Scranton branch hit Lake Scranton, America's eighth-largest indigenous body of water. Find your Lake Scranton. Encourage everyone to wear Hawaiian print to get into the right mindset for a day (and night) at the beach, and once you've hit the sand, bring out picnic tables and tiki torches. Provide Beach Necklaces (page 135) for all to wear. Feel free to use your Beach Day Journal (page 134) to take your own notes or to keep track of the winners for all the Funtivities (or a list of pros and cons).

Be sure to set up a Tabletop Tennis Table (page 137) or two, and provide paddles and balls for people to use. Set up a few snacks and the Hot Dog Bar (page 128) toppings while the hot dogs and veggies for the Firewalk Grilled Vegetables (page 132) are cooking, and then get ready for some fun in the sun!

"The mind has to wrap around the foot."
—Michael Scott

MICHAEL'S MANAGERIAL PRO & CON LISTS:

JIM:

Pros: Smart. Cool. Good-looking.

Cons: Not a hard worker.

DWIGHT:

Pros: Best sales record in the office.

Loves the work.

Cons: Idiot.

STANLEY:

Pros: All the good that black people have done for America.

ANDY:

Pros: Patriotic. Classy. Gets me.

Went to Cornell. I trust him.

Cons: I don't really trust him.

Casino Night

—Michael Scott

Willkommen. Bienvenue. And welcome to Casino Night! For one glamorous evening, Dunder Mifflin transformed their warehouse into a full-blown gambling hall where the stakes were high and the inhibitions were low. Their Casino Night was a really fun way to encourage friendly competition between coworkers, and you can easily do the same while also raising a lot of money for your favorite approved nonprofit organization. (You know, maybe something with animals. Or people.)

You can take inspiration from the lavish casinos of Monte Carlo or Las Vegas for your décor, and encourage your colleagues to play along by dressing up in fancy evening gowns and tuxedos (preferably not ones in which family members have been buried). Setting the right atmosphere goes a long way in making sure your fundraiser isn't a bust from the start. If it's an event you'd be proud to attend with a date—or possibly two—you know you've got yourself a winner.

Once the cards have all been dealt and the neon has faded, it'll be back to the daily grind for everyone. But for one night only, Lady Fortune is your boss, and she favors the bold—a fact Jim took to heart when he finally made a move that would change his and Pam's lives forever.

It doesn't matter whether you're attending with coworkers, old friends, or new lovers: At Casino Night, all are welcome. So leave your preconceived notions at the door, shuffle up, and deal!

FUN TIP:

Don't get carried away. Remember, Casino Night is supposed to be for a good cause. After a few wins, it's understandable that you might want to keep chasing that feeling, but you'll likely end up regretting it if the stakes get too high. Walking out with a mini fridge may seem like a major victory, but it's not a prize worth blowing your paycheck on.

Pizza Roulettes

As Dwight said, it's impossible to be an expert at roulette. It is, after all, a game of chance, not a game of skill. But if you want to look like an expert at something, you can always serve up these tasty roulette-themed pizza wheels. Just like the game from which they take their inspiration, these saucy spirals don't require a lot of skill—or mind control—to make, but the results are always a big win!

Prep Time: 45 minutes
Cook Time: 14 minutes
Yield: 24 pieces

One 11-ounce canister thin pizza dough
1 cup marinara sauce, plus more for serving
1½ cups shredded mozzarella
4 ounces pepperoni slices

1. Preheat the oven to 400°F. Remove the dough from the refrigerator and allow to warm slightly, but not fully to room temperature, for about 15 minutes.

2. On a lined baking sheet, roll out the pizza dough, and stretch by hand to approximately the size of the baking sheet.

3. Spread the marinara sauce on the dough, and then sprinkle the cheese evenly over the sauce, followed by the pepperoni. Starting on the long end of the baking sheet, carefully roll the dough into a log shape, and freeze the log on the pan for at least 30 minutes.

4. Remove the baking sheet from the freezer, and slice the log into ¼-inch-thick pinwheels. Lay them flat on the baking sheet, spaced at least 1 inch apart.

5. Bake for 12 to 14 minutes, until golden brown. Serve with more marinara for dipping.

NOTE: Freezing these helps the roulettes to retain their round shape when you cut them. If you want, assemble them in advance and leave them in the freezer, wrapped in plastic, until you're ready to bake and serve.

"I know it's illegal in Pennsylvania. But it's for charity."

—Michael Scott

"High Steaks" Kebabs

Want to go all in on your Casino Night cuisine? Then it's time to raise the *steaks*—in this case, marinated cubes of steak, grilled to perfection and served on convenient skewers. Hold one in your free hand while you play cards, roll dice, or sip on your favorite fancy cocktail. And when you're done, the skewer can be used to fend off anyone who tries to steal your extra chips!

Prep Time: 20 minutes, plus 2 or more hours marinating time
Cook Time: 10 minutes
Yield: 10 servings

FOR THE MARINADE:

1 cup olive oil
¼ cup red wine vinegar
1 tablespoon black pepper
1 tablespoon kosher salt
1 tablespoon garlic powder
1 tablespoon paprika
1 tablespoon red pepper flakes
2 teaspoons onion powder
2 teaspoons dried dill

FOR THE KEBABS:

1½ pounds sirloin steak, cut into 1-inch cubes
1 green bell pepper, cut into 1-inch squares
1 yellow bell pepper, cut into 1-inch squares
1 red onion, cut into 1-inch squares
20 cherry tomatoes
10 wooden skewers

1. Prepare the marinade. Combine all ingredients in a large resealable bag. Add steak cubes, making sure they're coated well, and refrigerate for at least 2 hours or up to overnight.

2. While the steak is marinating, soak the wooden skewers in water to reduce burning on the grill.

3. Preheat a grill over medium-high heat.

4. Prepare the kebabs. Alternate steak cubes with a few pieces of vegetables on each skewer. Drizzle any remaining marinade over the kebabs, paying extra attention to the vegetables.

5. Cook the kebabs on the grill, turning often, until steak has an internal temperature of about 145ºF for medium doneness, about 9 minutes. (Kebabs can also be baked in the oven at 425ºF for about 12 minutes.)

24-Karat Cocktail

Want to maximize the amount of cash you're raking in for the charity of your choice? Then make sure you're charging for drinks at the bar! While you can offer all the standards—beer, wine, and 7 and 7s with eight Maraschino cherries and sugar on the rim (in case someone orders Ryan's favorite drink)—you can really up the ante with a signature Casino Night cocktail that no one will be able to resist! This one sets the gold standard and is guaranteed to loosen up your coworkers (but probably not the slots).

Prep Time: 5 minutes
Yield: 1 serving

1 ounce spiced rum
¾ ounce cinnamon schnapps with gold flakes
Ginger beer
Lemon wedge

1. Fill a highball glass with ice. Add the rum and schnapps, and then fill the glass with ginger beer. Stir gently until mixed.

2. Garnish with a lemon wedge, and serve.

"I consider myself a great philanderer."
—Michael Scott

CRAFTS

Dice Decorations

Despite its somewhat off-putting name, craps can be an excellent group game and is a great way to get a crowd excited about an evening of gambling. You can bet these dice decorations will start your party off on a lucky streak that will have everyone cheering for you to "let it ride!"

SUPPLIES

- **Computer**
- **Printer**
- ⬇ **Dice Template**
- **White cardstock**
- **Tape**

1. Download and print the Dice Template from the online resources page onto a piece of white paper or cardstock.

2. Fold the dice sharply on the creases, and then place a piece of tape on the underside of the tabs and tape the tabs inside the dice.

3. Make a set of six for each table.

"We are giving money that has been gambled. Why don't we just deal drugs or prostitute ourselves and donate that money to charity?"

—Angela Martin

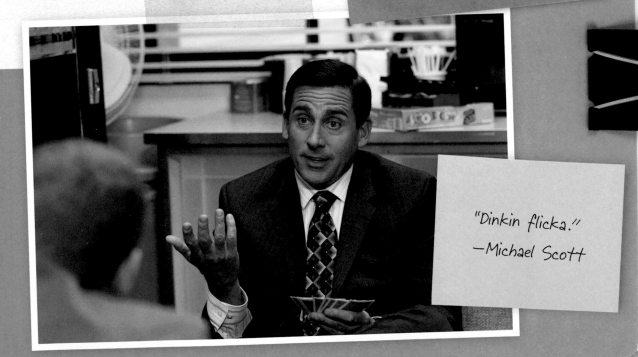

"Dinkin flicka."
—Michael Scott

Casino Sign

When fire-eaters aren't an option for your Casino Night—which, let's be honest, they probably shouldn't ever be—bright lights and sparkles can transform even the darkest warehouse into a Monte Carlo–inspired casino.

SUPPLIES

- **Shoe box or other similarly sized rectangular craft box**
- **White spray paint**
- **Black spray paint**
- **Clear green acrylic sheet (or other craft plastic sheet)**
- **Scissors**
- **Pencil**
- **Precision knife**
- **Cardboard**
- **Glue**
- **Battery-operated string of small LED lights**
- **Masking tape**

1. Take a shoe box or other craft box outside, and line the ground with cardboard to create a work surface. Spray-paint the interior of the box white. Let dry. Then spray-paint the exterior black. Let dry.

2. Cut the plastic sheet so it fits just inside the opening of the box.

3. Take a pencil and sketch out the word "CASINO" in block lettering on the cardboard. Be sure the letters will fit on the plastic sheet. Use the precision knife to cut out the letters, and then spray-paint the letters black. Let dry.

4. Glue the letters to the acrylic sheet so it reads "CASINO," lengthwise. Let dry.

5. Turn the box on its side, and tape the acrylic to the mouth of the cardboard box so it hangs down, covering the opening of the box with the word "CASINO" visible. Place the battery-operated string of lights inside the box. Make enough signs for the number of tables you plan to have.

Playing Card Bunting

One of your coworkers may or may not be the 2002 $2,500 No-Limit Deuce to Seven Draw Tournament champion at the World Series of Poker in Las Vegas, but you don't have to share his or her unconfirmed credentials to enjoy a good card game. Even if you can't tell a club from a clover, this simple card bunting will show off your two, or four, queens with this winning hand.

SUPPLIES
- **Hole punch**
- **Ribbon**
- **Deck of cards**

1. Use the hole punch to create 2 holes at the top of each card approximately 1½ inches apart.

2. String the cards onto the ribbon. Alternate suits and colors to create a pattern.

"Two queens on Casino Night. I am going to drop a deuce on everybody."

—Michael Scott

Special thanks to Bob Vance (Vance Refrigeration) for donating the mini refrigerator

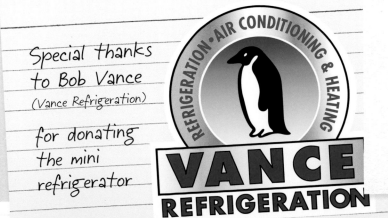

FUNTIVITIES

Casino Games

On the show, Angela felt it would be better to cut costs by having the Party Planning Committee volunteer to deal the cards, but Michael wanted to make sure that everyone got the chance to have some fun. Renting authentic casino games and hiring professional dealers to help facilitate the evening really helped provide a true Casino Night experience. Sure, it used up a good chunk of their budget, but it really made the event one to remember.

Select popular games that bring people together, such as poker, Texas Hold'em, pai gow, blackjack, craps, roulette, and more, and find out who is a secret card shark among your coworkers. Sometimes it's the person you'd least expect. Like Phyllis and Kevin. Who knew?

If you really want to entice players, offer a prize—like a mini fridge—to whoever has the most chips at the end of the evening.

DÉCOR

Situate the casino games and dealers around the room to allow enough space for people to play, and leave some room for others to watch in case gambling isn't their thing. Set up a number of tables where guests can eat, drink, and mingle in the center of the room, and cover those tables in green tablecloths or felt, if available, to give them that casino feel. And finally, put those classes to use as you assemble centerpieces using the Casino Signs (opposite page), Dice Decorations (page 145), additional playing cards, and poker chips.

Set up a table with the Pizza Roulettes (page 142), "High Steaks" Kebabs (page 143), 24-Karat Cocktails (page 144), and any other snacks or drinks you might like to include. Make multiple Playing Card Buntings, hang them around the room, and get ready for a night of gambling fun.

Halloween Party

> "I'm guessing Angela is the one in the neighborhood that gives the trick-or-treaters toothbrushes. Pennies. Walnuts."
>
> —Pam Beesly

Work can be pretty scary all year round, but at least there's one day a year where a bit of fear in the office can actually be a whole lot of fun: Halloween! November may be creeping up (as Erin says, can't stop that month!), but before it does, you've got one last chance to creep out your coworkers by playing off their deep-rooted fears of snakes, mummies, or, like Kelly, dying alone. So set the fog machine to medium, and be prepared . . . to be scared!

Office Halloween parties can go a lot of different ways, so it's important to know whether your workplace is having a simple spooky gathering or a full-blown Costume Celebration Spectacular. At the Scranton branch, they always rock what Andy would call some "sweet 'stumes," even though Corporate does not do Halloween (as Pam could attest). So know your company's culture when selecting a costume. There's nothing more awkward than showing up to work dressed like Charlie Chaplin when everyone else is sporting standard business attire.

When deciding on your costume, do your best to think outside the box so you don't all end up dressing like the Joker or something. While vampire, hobo, and cat costumes are classic fun, there are so many unique outfit options to choose from. Make yourself a second head out of papier-mâché like Michael, invent a superhero that represents your company like Kevin did, or even dress as a local serial killer like Dwight (who, to be fair, may or may not actually be a local serial killer). Just try not to be offensive or cliché. And don't dress up as one of your coworkers. (It never goes well.)

If Halloween really isn't your thing, Jim had a bunch of low-key costume ideas that allowed him to join in on the fun without ever looking like he was trying too hard. If even that is too much effort for you, you can always just stay at your desk and pull on a monster mask like Stanley. Hopefully, everyone will be having too much fun to notice that you're napping through the festivities.

FUN TIP:

Play it safe. Dressing up creatively is absolutely encouraged at an office Halloween party, but to guarantee the safety of everyone attending, certain areas of authenticity need to be sacrificed. Like Toby needed to tell Dwight every year: You can't bring weapons into the office. It's basic common sense, as long as you're not Dwight apparently.

Kevin's Famous Chili

Kevin's legendary family recipe has been passed down by Malones for generations. This chili is some serious stuff. You can save some valuable prep time by buying pre-pressed garlic, pre-diced tomatoes, and pre-toasted ancho chilies, as long as you remember that the real trick is to undercook the onions. As Kevin says, everybody will get to know one another in the pot . . . and hopefully not on the carpet . . .

"It's probably the thing I do best."
—Kevin Malone

Prep Time: 15 minutes
Cook Time: 2 hours
Yield: 8 servings

2 medium poblano peppers
¼ cup neutral cooking oil
2 pounds ground beef
2 large yellow onions, chopped
6 cloves garlic, minced or pressed through a garlic press
2 tablespoons chili powder
1 teaspoon dried oregano
1 teaspoon black pepper
1 teaspoon cayenne pepper
1 teaspoon smoked paprika
1 bay leaf
1 teaspoon ground chipotle peppers (optional)
¼ cup tomato paste
One 28-ounce can chopped tomatoes
Two 15-ounce cans pinto beans
One 12-ounce can dark beer
1 tablespoon bittersweet chocolate chips

OPTIONAL GARNISHES: shredded cheddar cheese, sour cream, minced raw onion, avocado, chopped fresh cilantro

1. Wearing plastic gloves, prepare the poblano peppers. Wash and pat them dry, and then roast the peppers. This can be done in two ways: Either roast the peppers over an open flame on a gas stove burner, using tongs to rotate them until blackened on all sides; or roast them under a broiler in the oven, rotating every minute or so until blackened on all sides. Either method should take about 5 minutes. When the peppers are cool enough to handle, peel off the skin, and discard. Slice the peppers in half, discard the stems and seeds, and dice the rest.

2. In a large, heavy-bottomed stockpot, heat the cooking oil over medium-high heat. Add the ground beef, and cook until browned, about 8 minutes. Use a slotted spoon to remove the meat to a bowl, and set aside. If there is a lot of grease in the pan, drain the grease but leave a few tablespoons in the pan for the next step.

3. In the same pot, add the onion and garlic. Cook over medium-high heat until just starting to soften but still slightly undercooked, about 6 minutes. Add the chili powder, oregano, black pepper, cayenne pepper, smoked paprika, bay leaf, and ground chipotle peppers, if using. Stir well and cook 2 minutes. Add the tomato paste and ground beef, then cook another 10 minutes.

4. Add the tomatoes, beans, beer, poblanos, and chocolate chips. Simmer for about 90 minutes, until the flavors are totally combined. Adjust spice level to taste. Serve with the garnishes of your choice.

Bacon-Wrapped Grilled Asparagus

If you're the kind of person who loves waking up to the smell of bacon, your mouth will water for these sizzling spears. Fortunately, for those of us who don't have butlers, they're easy to prepare on an indoor electric grill. For safety reasons, do not sleep while preparing this dish or place the electric grill anywhere you could step on it.

Prep Time: 5 minutes
Cook Time: 10 minutes
Yield: 10 servings

1 pound thin-stalked asparagus
Salt and black pepper, to taste
10 slices bacon
2 tablespoons olive oil

1. Rinse asparagus, and cut the hard end off the bottom of each stalk, usually about 2 to 3 inches. Season with salt and pepper.

2. Divide the asparagus into 10 bundles of about 3 stalks each. Wrap each bundle with a slice of bacon.

3. In a large skillet, heat the olive oil. Cook the bundles in two batches, browning the bacon on all sides, until the asparagus is bright green and starting to soften and the bacon is completely cooked, about 10 minutes. Remove to paper towels to drain, if necessary, and serve.

"Halloween should be a day in which we honor monsters and not be mad at each other."

—Michael Scott

Pretzel Day Pretzels

When you work a job where you get paid too little, sometimes it's the simple joys that make the biggest difference, like a complimentary soft pretzel. The Scranton branch's office building had its annual Pretzel Day every April. Your office may not be so lucky, so enjoy this recipe included here. While you could go the traditional salted route, a sweet pretzel with a cinnamon-sugar coating and a warm chocolate dip is a treat worth waiting in line for any day of the year.

Prep Time: 40 minutes
Cook Time: 12 minutes
Yield: 30 pieces

3 cups all-purpose flour, plus more for kneading surface
1 cup plus 2 tablespoons granulated sugar, divided
2 tablespoons packed light brown sugar
1 teaspoon salt
1 packet instant yeast
3½ cups water, divided
2 tablespoons vegetable oil
¼ cup baking soda
½ cup (1 stick) salted butter
1 tablespoon cinnamon

1. Combine 3 cups flour, 2 tablespoons granulated sugar, brown sugar, salt, and yeast in a large bowl.

2. Combine 1 cup water and the 2 tablespoons vegetable oil in a medium saucepan over high heat until warm. Remove the pan from heat and add to the flour mixture in small increments until fully incorporated into a soft dough.

3. On a floured surface, knead the dough for about 5 minutes, until smooth and elastic. Cover and let rest for 10 minutes.

4. Preheat the oven to 425°F.

5. Separate the dough into 8 equal sections, and then roll out each section into a rope about 12 to 14 inches long. Cut each rope into 3 or 4 roughly equal pieces. Cover and allow to rest for another 10 minutes.

6. Heat the remaining 2½ cups of water so it is hot, then dissolve the baking soda in the water. Dip each piece of dough into the water, and then place on a lined baking sheet.

7. Bake for about 12 minutes, until light brown. Allow to cool slightly.

8. In a small skillet over medium heat, melt the butter. Remove from the heat.

9. In a medium bowl, combine the remaining granulated sugar and cinnamon. Dip each pretzel stick into the butter, and then roll in the sugar mixture to coat. Serve warm.

Orange Vod-Juice-Ka

Michael thought he was a master mixologist, with inspired creations like the Orange Vod-Juice-Ka to his name. This would blow him away—a delicious twist on his "original" creation. It might not be an elaborate witch's brew, but this easy cocktail is perfect for the office party where the spooky decorations and costume contest prizes already ate up most of the planning budget. Luckily, this one is so tasty that you won't believe no one thought of it sooner! (They did.)

Prep Time: 5 minutes
Yield: 1 serving

2 ounces vodka
1 ounce orange liqueur, preferably Cointreau
Juice of 1 mandarin or tangerine
Tonic water
Twist of orange peel, for garnish

1. Fill a highball glass with ice.

2. Add the vodka, liqueur, and juice. Fill to the top with tonic water, and stir well. Garnish with orange peel, and serve.

"Fear plays an interesting role in our lives. How dare we let it motivate us? How dare we let it into our decision-making, into our livelihoods, into our relationships? It's funny, isn't it, we take a day a year to dress up in costume and celebrate fear?"

—Robert California

Pin the Wart on the Witch

Some of your guests—possibly your CEO's preteen son—might think that party games are for babies. Even though Pin the Wart on the Witch might seem a little "kiddie," maybe it's the kind of game that can wake up the baby in all of us. Just give it a chance, okay, because no one wants to make your new receptionist cry.

SUPPLIES

- **Scissors**
- **Black, gray, green, and dark green (or other contrasting color) felt**
- **Hot-glue gun**
- **Permanent marker**
- **Packet of ½-inch or ⅝-inch circular hook and loop dots with adhesive backings**

1. Use the scissors to cut out the following shapes:
   - **Black felt: witch's hat**
   - **Green felt: egg-shaped face and triangular nose**
   - **Yellow felt: ½-inch-by-4-inch-wide rectangles (8 to 12 pieces)**
   - **Dark green (or contrasting color) felt: 1-inch-wide circles**

2. Using the hot-glue gun, attach the hat to the top of the face.

3. Turn over the hat and face, and glue the rectangles as hair, sticking out from under the hat.

4. Flip back to the front side. Attach the nose in the appropriate location using the hot-glue gun.

5. Outline the nose in permanent marker, and hand-draw the eyes and mouth on the witch. This is your opportunity to have fun and personalize your witch! Make her as spooky or as fun as you'd like.

6. Remove the adhesive back from the "hook" or "teeth" sides of the dots, and attach it to one of the dark green felt circles. These will be the warts for your game.

"It turns out Pam really, really hates 'Monster Mash.' I mean, like, never bring that song up in front of her. Even though Jim was making great points, like, in favor of the song, Pam was like, 'No. Hate it. Stupid.'"

—Kevin Malone

DUNDER MIFFLIN INC,
PAPER COMPANY

1725 SLOUGH AVENUE
SCRANTON, PA 18505

"Happy Halloween! How can I haunt you today?"
—Erin Hannon

"So, can we speak our minds now, or are we still sparing feelings, because I hate all of this."
—Angela Martin

Personalize Your Cat Costume

Throughout the years, the Dunder Mifflin office celebrated countless Halloweens, and many of them have featured office cats showing off their personal style. From Angela's pristine white cat outfit to Andy's musical-inspired cat, the sky's the limit when it comes to designing your favorite at costume.

SUPPLIES

- **Faux-fur fabric or trim, or other plush fabric such as fleece**
- **Pipe cleaners or thicker-gauge craft wire**
- **Hot-glue gun**
- **Headband**
- **Safety pin**
- **Sewing needle**
- **Scissors**
- **Cotton stuffing**

CAT EARS INSTRUCTIONS

1. Select your favorite cat to imitate, and choose the appropriate colored faux fur or fleece and pipe cleaners.

2. Bend the pipe cleaners into triangles to create a frame for the ears. Use the hot-glue gun to glue the pipe cleaners to the headband.

3. Cut the faux fur or fleece to fit the ear, and use hot-glue gun to attach the ear to the pipe cleaner.

4. Put aside to set before wearing.

CAT TAIL INSTRUCTIONS

1. Decide how long you want your tail to be, and cut a 4-inch wide strip of faux fur or fleece at that length.

2. Measure pipe cleaners or craft wire the same length as the fabric strip. Twist pipe cleaners together if the tail is longer than a single pipe cleaner.

3. Fold the fabric in half with the "outside," or "design side," of the fabric facing in. Use a basic running stitch to sew a seam up the side. When you get to the end, sew a diagonal to give the tail a point, and tie off the thread. Turn the fabric right side out so the design is now facing out.

4. Place the pipe cleaner inside the fabric tube. This is what will give your tail its shape. Fill the tail with cotton stuffing, making sure the tail is filled all the way to the tip.

5. Sew the end of the tail closed, and shape as you wish.

6. Use a safety pin to attach the tail to the rest of your costume.

TIP: Complete the look with face paint by properly drawing a nose and whiskers as part of the finishing touches.

"You can't change costumes in the middle of the day!"
—Angela Martin

3-Hole-Punch Jim Costume

Take a break from being your boring, plain self and instead become an ultracool three-hole punch version . . . of yourself. This simple-yet-memorable outfit was Jim's perfect way to show he had a costume while also letting everyone know that he really didn't care about dressing up at all. Pure elegance.

SUPPLIES

- **Black felt**
- **Scissors**
- **Tape**
- **Button-up white shirt**

1. Cut three circles the same size from the black felt.

2. Using tape, attach the circles to your shirt approximately 2 inches apart.

3. Show disinterest in the rest of the partygoers' costumes.

"We are doing a haunted house this Halloween, which is actually kind of spooky, because as legend has it, on this very site, there used to be a productive paper company."

—Jim Halpert

Door Drapes

Ready to give your Halloween party some extra *pizzazz*? Door Drapes are the spookiest way to add some darkness to your party decor. Well, at least, the spookiest item we're legally allowed to bring into an office building.

SUPPLIES

- **Black plastic tablecloth(s)**
- **Scissors**
- **Tape**

1. Tape the tablecloth to the top of the doorframe, and straighten it out. If it is longer or wider than the door, cut to fit.

2. Using scissors, cut long vertical strips that are 1 to 2 inches wide. Continue until the entire tablecloth is in tatters.

3. Repeat with other doors, and "be prepared to be scared."

"How many freakin' vampires am I supposed to care about these days?"
—Stanley Hudson

Insane Asylum Sign

Have your coworkers been driving you nuts all year? This easy-to-make wooden Insane Asylum Sign will show them how you feel about them. Of course, if they ask, you can always just say you made it as a reminder of how crazy Halloween can get, especially if you have a boss like Michael. Either way, when it comes to fun, this craft will show exactly how *committed* you are.

SUPPLIES

- **Drill and drill bit**
- **Precut wooden sign from the craft store in whatever size you would like**
- **Acrylic paint and paintbrush**
- **Computer**
- **⬇ Insane Asylum Stencil Template**
- **Printer**
- **Tape**
- **Pencil or pen**
- **Twine**

1. Drill two holes at the top of the wooden sign that are approximately 2 to 3 inches apart. The spacing will vary based on the size of the sign you choose.

2. Paint the front and back of the sign black. Let dry.

3. Download and print the Insane Asylum Stencil Template from the online resources page.

4. Once the sign is fully dry, center the stencil on the front of the sign and tape it down. You do not need to cut out the letters.

5. Using a pen or pencil, firmly draw around the edges of the letters on the stencil. Be sure to use enough pressure to leave a mark in the sign beneath. When you lift the stencil, you should be able to clearly see the design in the wood.

6. Paint inside the "Insane Asylum" design with white, yellow, or red paint.

7. Thread twine through the drilled holes, and hang the sign.

FUNTIVITIES

Pin the Wart on the Witch

Appealing to everyone's sensibilities is a delicate balance. Sometimes we forget that Halloween is a chance to let out your inner kid and have fun. You may feel pressure to grow your party up real fast, but before you send your little kid party to clean its room, consider this: Most people, even the adults, would much rather play a game of Pin the Wart on the Witch than a hand of Pecker Poker any day of the year.

While the game can be enjoyed by players of any age, the rules are easy enough for even the youngest guests. Blindfold your first contestant with a tie, and have them spin around the same number of times as their age—or just five times, if you don't want to be mean.

Face them in the direction of the witch, and hand them a wart. Players must walk toward the witch, and place the wart against the witch's face without feeling for the nose. The person who gets closest to the nose wins.

Costume Contest Voting

Even though everyone tends to come to work in costume on Halloween, for every Kelly who is ready to strut their stuff there's an Angela who would rather stay in the background. A prize—like the Scranton/Wilkes-Barre Coupon Book, worth over $15,000 in savings—can be a real motivator to get people into the spirit of the occasion. Even the Stanley of your office, believe it or not! So turn on some music, clear the runway, and try not to think about the prize's actual value, as your fellow partygoers show off their best dance moves in character.

Distribute index cards to the attendees, and have them vote for who is the best dressed at the party. The costume with the most votes wins!

> "If I have to vote for someone, I don't want it to be someone who can beat me."
> —Kelly Kapoor

DÉCOR

The spookiest day of the year is the best time to go all out with decorations. To give your party flavor that everyone enjoys, divide the room into scary and non-scary sides.

On the scary side, dim the lights, and bring in a fog machine to give the room ambience. Hang photos of the scariest creatures you can find.

On the non-scary side, create a look that would be better suited for an elementary school classroom. Hang your Pin the Wart on the Witch (page 156) game on the wall so everyone can play the game in the kid-friendly section.

Cartoon witches, cats, bats, and pumpkins are always crowd favorites for wall decor, and Halloween string lights are a fun touch. Add Door Drapes (page 162) to all the doorways, and make sure to put your Insane Asylum Sign (page 162) in a place of pride to remind everyone how crazy this party can be.

Prank

Want to really get into the spirit of Halloween? You could always follow Dwight's example by cutting the bottom out of a pumpkin and using it as a mask to scare your friends! Make sure to cut the hole large enough that you can get the pumpkin back off your head later, or it may be the costliest decision you've ever made. After all, as Jim and Dwight discovered, any blow to the pumpkin itself could prove fatal to the person wearing it. Thankfully, worst-case scenario, the pumpkin should rot off in a month or two.

Holiday Party

"Christmas isn't about Santa or Jesus. It's about the workplace."

—Michael Scott

As the end of the calendar year approaches, it's the perfect time for you and your office to look back and reflect on everything you've accomplished together as a team. Dunder Mifflin was always so much more than just a company. It was a family. And just like a family, sometimes they disagreed, they fought, and they made mistakes. But they all knew deep down that they loved, respected, and needed one another. There was no better time than their annual Holiday Party to come together, put aside their differences, and celebrate what makes each of them so special—in the form of gifts under $20.

It's been said that presents are the best way to show someone how much you care, but no one expects their Secret Santa to buy them diamonds and brooch pendants. For your holiday party, try to find something fun that you can get for under $20, like a teapot, a poster of babies dressed as adults, or a portable video player from 2005. A personalized or homemade gift is also a wonderful way to show you care. (Unless it's an oven mitt.)

Once the gifts are wrapped, we'll need a place to put them. If you're planning on putting up a tree, choose one that will fit appropriately in the office (and your hybrid car). If it's too tall, just lop off the top with a paper cutter, and you'll have a perfectly good mini-tree to sell to charity! Once decorated, watch the wonder (or disappointment) in our coworkers' eyes as you unveil your hard work to them.

Whether you celebrate Christmas, Hanukkah, or Pancha Ganapati at home, use the first part of your corporate-sanctioned half-day off to celebrate what really matters: each other.

FUN TIP:

Keep it simple, Santa! Having an office gift exchange is great, but things can get overly complicated and extremely frustrating for everyone participating if you start switching up the rules midstream. Whether you decide to go with a straightforward Secret Santa or play a Yankee Swap game (page 184), make sure everyone has a clear understanding of the exchange process and try not to deviate. No one wants to see a heartwarming activity spiral into complete chaos. Not even Belsnickel.

Andy's Holiday Cheese Board

If you're looking for a classic and classy way to kick off any party, you can always count on a cheese plate. Andy seems to think that a nice firm cheddar paired with a cheddar-style spread is a perfectly acceptable assortment, but there are plenty of other fancier cheeses out there that are both challenging and delicious. So be creative, and try to add something bold and new to your selection. Oh, and blue cheese dressing definitely doesn't count, even if there are fish-shaped crackers swimming in it.

Prep Time: 5 minutes
Yield: 8 servings as an appetizer

One 4- to 6-ounce wedge hard cheese, such as Parmesan or Gruyère

One 4- to 6-ounce wedge stronger flavored hard cheese, such as smoked gouda or aged cheddar

One 4- to 6-ounce wedge soft cheese, such as Brie or goat cheese

One 4- to 6-ounce wedge blue-veined cheese, such as blue cheese or gorgonzola

1 cup Marcona almonds, or other nuts

1 cup dried apricots or other dehydrated fruit

1 cup marinated, mixed olives

½ cup sweet fruit spread, such as quince paste or fig preserves

1. Unwrap all cheeses, and arrange on a large platter, with space between each cheese.

2. Put your fruit spread and olives in small bowls or ramekins, and place on the platter in the center.

3. Fill in the spaces with the fruit and nuts. Serve.

NOTE: The beauty of a cheese plate is that you can get as creative as you want. Just make sure that you have a variety of textures and flavors of cheese—make sure some cheeses are hard and some are soft, and some have sharp flavors and some mellow. Add any combination of salty complements, like olives and nuts, and sweet ones, like dried or fresh fruit that you like. Smart hosts will reserve half of each cheese to replenish the plate later in the party, so that none of the perishable elements are sitting out too long.

"I decided to give Erin the Twelve Days of Christmas. Is it my fault that the first eight days there's basically 30 birds?"

—Andy Bernard

Moroccan Christmas Mezze Platter

Tired of having the same tacky deli platter food every year? So was Phyllis. The year she was head of the Party Planning Committee, she solved that problem by putting together a totally unique Moroccan-themed Christmas bash. This unforgettable event spiced up our season's eatings with a variety of Middle Eastern delicacies, including hummus, falafel, and little triangles of pita. This isn't your grandmother's holiday party spread! (Unless, of course, she's from Morocco, in which case it's very accurate.)

Prep Time: 15 minutes
Yield: 10 servings

FOR THE MEZZE PLATTER:

Hummus (see recipe below)
Tzatziki (see recipe below)
One 16-ounce jar roasted red peppers
One 12-ounce jar marinated artichoke hearts
1 cup spicy marinated olives
2 cups crumbled or cubed feta cheese
2 cups cooked couscous
6 large pitas, cut into 8 wedges each

FOR THE TZATZIKI:

1 large cucumber
2 tablespoons fresh dill
1 clove garlic
2 tablespoons lemon juice
½ teaspoon salt
¼ teaspoon black pepper
1 cup plain Greek yogurt

FOR THE HUMMUS:

One 15-ounce can chickpeas, drained
Juice of 1 lemon
¼ cup tahini
1 clove garlic
1 teaspoon salt
½ teaspoon black pepper
¼ cup olive oil

1. Prepare the tzatziki. Cut the cucumber into several large chunks, discarding the ends. Pulse in a food processor until roughly chopped but not pureed. Remove to a strainer and allow to drain of excess liquid.

2. In the food processor, add the remaining ingredients, and pulse to fully combine. Remove the mixture to a medium glass bowl, and then add the cucumber. Stir to combine, and refrigerate for at least 1 hour to allow flavors to meld. Remove to a small serving bowl.

3. Prepare the hummus. Place the chickpeas, lemon, tahini, garlic, salt, and pepper into a food processor. Pulse a few times. Then, with the machine running on low, slowly pour the olive oil into the mixture until the hummus becomes smooth and silky. You may not need the entire ¼ cup. Adjust the seasonings to taste. If desired, add fresh herbs, more lemon juice, or more garlic to make a flavored hummus. Remove to a small serving bowl.

4. Prepare the mezze platter. Place the bowls of hummus and tzatziki in the middle of a large platter, and then add the peppers, artichoke hearts, olives, feta, and couscous to fill in around the bowls. Serve with pita wedges for dipping.

Angela's Double-Fudge Brownies

Even the joys of the holiday season can't salvage a boring office party. But you know what can? Double-fudge brownies. Angela's brownie recipe is so rich and decadent that most of her coworkers barely even noticed how much her party paled in comparison to the competing party down the hall with margaritas, karaoke, and a raffle.

Prep Time: 10 minutes
Cook Time: 25 minutes
Yield: 24 brownies

Nonstick cooking spray
1 cup (2 sticks) unsalted butter, melted and cooled
2 cups sugar
2 tablespoons vanilla extract
3 large eggs
1 cup all-purpose flour
1 cup dark cocoa powder
1 teaspoon salt
1 cup chocolate chips

1. Preheat the oven to 325°F.

2. Spray the inside of a 9-by-13-inch baking pan with nonstick cooking spray.

3. Prepare the brownies. In a large mixing bowl, whisk the butter and sugar together. Add the vanilla and eggs, and stir to combine.

4. Add the remaining ingredients, and stir until just mixed.

5. Pour the batter into the baking pan, and bake until a knife inserted into the center of the pan comes out not quite clean but not fully coated in batter, about 35 to 40 minutes. Remove from the oven and allow to cool for 10 to 15 minutes. Cut into squares, and serve.

One-of-Anything Christmas Punch

Michael created his infamous "One of Everything" by mixing together equal parts scotch, absinthe, rum, gin, vermouth, triple sec, and two packs of sugar substitute. Unfortunately, Meredith loved it a little too much . . . so in order to avoid future fire hazards, try this nonalcoholic "One of Anything" punch in its place. To be fair, it tastes great on its own, but it also makes a fantastic mixer for a shot of any spirit you've got. So if you happen to have any rum, bourbon, vodka, gin, or tequila handy, your coworkers can spike their punch how they see fit.

Prep Time: 12 hours 10 minutes (10 minutes active, 12 hours freeze time)
Yield: 20 servings

FOR THE ROSEMARY SIMPLE SYRUP:

1 cup sugar
1 cup water
2 sprigs rosemary

FOR THE CHRISTMAS ICE CUBES:

30 to 40 cranberries
2 sprigs rosemary

FOR THE PUNCH:

2 trays plain ice cubes
8 cups 100 percent cranberry juice
4 cups ginger ale
One 750-milliliter-bottle sparkling cider
1 cup Rosemary Simple Syrup
2 trays Christmas Ice Cubes
1 cup cranberries
1 orange, sliced into wheels

1. Prepare the Rosemary Simple Syrup. In a small saucepan over high heat, bring the sugar and water to a boil. Remove from the heat, add the rosemary, and allow to steep for at least 1 hour. Remove the rosemary before using.

2. Prepare the Christmas Ice Cubes. In each well of 2 ice cube trays, place 1 cranberry and 1 small snippet of a rosemary sprig (2 to 3 needles, still attached to the stem). Fill with water, and freeze overnight.

3. Prepare the punch. In a large punch bowl, add 2 trays of plain ice. Add all the liquids, and stir well to combine. Place the Christmas Ice Cubes, cranberries, and orange slices on top to float.

RECEPTION

CRAFTS

Paper Snowflakes

Dwight may be too cynical to find the magic in the first snowfall of Christmas, but there's something about a winter wonderland that really does make you want to have a hot chocolate and cuddle up with someone you love. Even though it's not real snow, these Paper Snowflakes are an easy way to bring your Christmas dreams to life indoors.

SUPPLIES

- **8½-by-11-inch printer paper**
- **Scissors**
- **Tape or fishing wire**

1. Cut several pieces of printer paper into a square by removing 2½ inches from the long side. You will want as many squares of paper as the number of snowflakes you wish to create.

2. Work one at a time, and fold each square in half diagonally.

3. Fold each square in half a second time to make a small triangle.

4. Fold the small triangles into thirds by folding the two folded sides in toward each other. The bottom should now look like an open V.

5. Flip the V over then fold the two side together one more time.

6. Using a pair of scissors, cut off the top.

7. Cut random shapes from the triangle. Unfold to reveal your snowflake.

8. To display, either tape the snowflakes on the walls or hang from the ceiling with fishing wire.

9. Repeat for the number of snowflakes you wish to display.

"Somebody really got carried away with the Spirit of Christmas. It was me."

—Michael Scott

1

2

3

4 flip

5

6

7

Holiday Card Photo Frame

Everyone enjoys getting Christmas cards, especially ones with pictures of their closest friends and family . . . or in Michael's case, someone else's family. That's definitely not the best way to go, but you can still give the people on your mailing list that same awkward feeling by sending them a seasonal photo of the entire staff wearing Santa hats while jumping in the air or doing a *Charlie's Angels* pose. Sure, it's just a card from a local business, but if someone does decide to put it on their fridge, you and your team might as well look nice.

"Happy Birthday, Jesus. Sorry your party's so lame."

—Michael Scott

SUPPLIES

- **Cardstock**
- **Patterned holiday paper**
- **Group photo printed at 5-by-7**
- **Precision knife**
- **Self-healing mat or cardboard**

1. Place the cardstock you wish to use for the backside of the frame on top of the self-healing mat or cardboard. This is to protect your tabletop as you cut.

2. Using a precision knife, cut a 6½-by-8½-inch rectangle out of the cardstock. Set the cardstock aside.

3. Place the holiday paper on the cardboard or mat.

4. Using a precision knife, cut a 6-by-8-inch rectangle.

5. In the center of the rectangle you just cut, cut another rectangle that is 4¾ inches by 6½ inches.

6. Use a glue stick to place a thin, ¼-inch line of glue along the backside of the top of the patterned rectangle. Attach the glue side to the cardstock, lining it up.

7. Slide a 5-by-7 photo into the frame. If necessary, tape the edges of the photo inside the frame so it stays in place.

Holiday Garland

Holiday decorations are the perfect way to bring some cheer to a dreary office. Take a coffee break, and spend some time assembling a Holiday Garland using your favorite decorative paper and a pair of fun-edged scrapbook scissors.

SUPPLIES
- **Red and green (or other colors of preference) decorative paper**
- **Hot-glue gun**
- **Fun-edged scrapbook scissors**
- **Tape**

1. Using scrapbook scissors, cut the paper into 1½-by-8½-inch strips. If you use standard decorative paper, this will result in 7 strips per sheet.

2. Place a dab of hot glue on one short end and roll the paper into a loop to glue together. Be careful not to glue your fingers in the process.

3. Alternating colors, loop the next paper through the circle you just created, and glue the end in the same manner. This should create a chain.

4. Repeat until your chain is the length you wish to display. Hang the garland around the room or around the edge of the food table with tape.

Princess Unicorn Horn

No one wants to be the parent who missed out on the hottest gift of the season, and some, like Toby, will go to drastic measures to make sure they get to be the hero in their little girl's life for once. If you forgot to buy a Princess Unicorn Doll, you don't have to cave in and pay the insane prices that the Dwights of the world are asking for. Why not light up your princess's face when you tell her she gets to *be* Princess Unicorn instead, thanks to this handmade horn? It might not be exactly what she wanted, but at least you'll save a few hundred dollars to buy her something better on her birthday.

SUPPLIES:

- ⬇ **Princess Unicorn Horn Template**
- **Scissors**
- **Store-bought princess crown**
- **One 9-by-12-inch sheet of white felt**
- **Polyfill stuffing**
- **Hot-glue gun**
- **Gold embroidery floss**
- **Pencil**
- **Colored ribbons (optional)**

1. Print out the Princess Unicorn Horn Template from the online resources page. Cut out the template paper pieces for the horn and base, and place on top of your felt sheet. Trace around the template pieces, and cut one of each out of the felt.

2. Use the hot-glue gun to apply glue along the long edge of the horn piece, noted on the template. Overlap the two edges by about ¼-inch, and press together for a few seconds for the glue to adhere. The horn should form a slanted oval shape at the bottom once wrapped, which will help it point upward when attached to the crown.

3. Stuff the horn with a pinch of stuffing at a time, gently pushing it into the tip of the horn with a pencil.

4. Once the horn is stuffed, apply hot glue on the bottom of the rim of the horn, and press on the circle of the base felt.

5. Place a dot of hot glue on the base of the horn, and press one end of your gold embroidery floss on it. Wrap the floss around and up to the tip of the horn, and place a hot-glue dot to the tip to attach the floss. Trim excess floss.

6. Apply hot glue to the base of the horn and attach to the center of the crown front. Be sure the horn is pointed upward to pierce the sky.

7. If you like, you can make it even sparklier by attaching ribbons to the sides of the crown headband.

"That's what every boss wants, is a wonderful Christmas with no drama."
—Michael Scott

176

Homemade Oven Mitt

Michael has made it clear that presents should be something that you are able to point to and say, "Hey, man, I love you this many dollars worth." But many believe that handcrafted gifts are still a lovely gesture, particularly when they're both fashionable and functional. A gift from the heart like this oven mitt is something no one could ever replace. Even though they might do everything in their power to try. If you don't know how to knit like Phyllis, it's easy to hand sew an oven mitt instead.

NOTE: This mitt (and Phyllis's knit creation) is for craft purposes only. Do not use this oven mitt as an actual oven mitt, or you could get burned worse than Michael's foot on an indoor grill.

SUPPLIES

- **Brown paper bag**
- **Cotton fabric**
- **Insulated batting**
- **Sewing thread and a needle**
- **Fabric scissors**

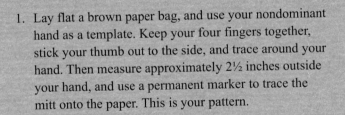

1. Lay flat a brown paper bag, and use your nondominant hand as a template. Keep your four fingers together, stick your thumb out to the side, and trace around your hand. Then measure approximately 2½ inches outside your hand, and use a permanent marker to trace the mitt onto the paper. This is your pattern.

2. Use the paper pattern to cut 4 pieces of cotton fabric and 2 pieces of insulated batting.

3. Lay 2 pieces of cotton fabric cutouts together with the pattern facing out on both sides. Insert 1 piece of batting between the 2 cotton pieces.

4. Use a sewing needle and thread (or sewing machine if you have it) to sew 4 lines of running stitch diagonally across the mitt. Each line should be spaced out approximately 1 inch from one another, or evenly across the mitt.

5. Repeat steps 3 and 4 for the other two pieces of fabric and batting.

6. On the bottom of each mitt (the flat part), use a blanket stitch to close the end of the fabric. You may wish to use a contrasting piece of embroidery thread for this step.

7. Place the two sides together and use a running stitch to sew around the outside (curved) side of the mitt.

8. Turn the project inside out, and you're done.

"I know you did a lot to help this year but I only care about you a homemade oven mitt's worth."
—Michael Scott

DIY Teapot Gift

Back before they started dating, Jim put together a special gift for Pam as part of their Secret Santa gift exchange . . . and then she immediately traded it for a portable media player. Of course, at the time, she had no idea how much thought he had put into it. The teapot was filled with bonus gifts that not only showed how well he knew her, but also how much they already meant to each other. It ended up being one of Pam's favorite gifts ever. Try this for someone you really care about.

SUPPLIES

- **Teapot**
- **Cassette tape (if you can find one) or a flash drive loaded with music**
- **Photocopied yearbook photo**
- **Boggle timer**
- **Golf pencil**
- **Hot sauce packet**
- **Your own personal inside jokes**
- **Tissue paper**
- **Gift box**

1. Assemble all your supplies, including recording all your favorite songs on a cassette or downloading them to a flash drive.

2. Fill the teapot with the small gifts.

3. Wrap the teapot in tissue paper and place into a gift box.

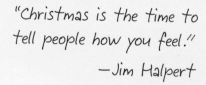

"Christmas is the time to tell people how you feel."

—Jim Halpert

180

Belsnickel Costume

Who needs St. Nicholas when you could have Belsnickel—his crotchety, fur-clad, gift-giving companion from the folklore of Southwestern Germany? So like Santa, but dirty and worse. According to Dwight, in a head-to-head contest, people prefer Belsnickel over Santa every time. Though, I'd really like to see some data to support that. Still, if you'd like to bring some authority and fear to your holiday gathering, be sure to dress the part, and remember, Belsnickel is still judging your year—so be admirable, not impish!

SUPPLIES

- **Black felt or faux fur hat**
- **Twigs and leaves**
- **Hot-glue gun**
- **Brown costume beard**
- **Several yards faux fur, muslin, and/or burlap fabric**
- **Long, thin sticks**
- **Thick brown belt or rope**
- **String**
- **Whip**
- **Burlap sack**

1. Hot glue the twigs and leaves haphazardly to the felt hat. Let cool.

2. Wrap the faux fur (or muslin or burlap) over your shoulders, and wrap around twice to form a sort of coat. Tie at the waist with the brown belt or rope.

3. Gather the thin sticks in a bundle, and tie the string around the bottom of the bundle to keep them together while you wave them at your coworkers.

4. Don the felt hat and brown beard and carry the sticks, whip, and burlap sack.

5. Play Impish or Admirable (page 182).

FUNTIVITIES

Impish or Admirable?

According to Dwight, nothing brings more joy to a holiday celebration than having some darkly erotic freak judge who's the least deserving of gifts. Whether you're creeped out by Belsnickel or genuinely confused, it's probably best for everyone to just play along. All you need to do is provide each guest with a bowl, and instruct them to sit in a circle. Belsnickel will take it from there.

TIP: Before playing, make a list and check it twice.

As you go around the circle, the person dressed as Belsnickle must state the following rhyme as they announce who is impish or admirable.

"CHEER OR FEAR, BELSNICKEL IS HERE, I JUDGE YOUR YEAR AS 'IMPISH / ADMIRABLE.'"

Admirable guests should receive gifts (ideally not mousetraps) while impish guests get a rap with the sticks.

Poetry Readings

There's something peaceful about having a seasonal poem read out loud at Christmas . . . unless that poem is German and nobody in your office speaks that language. In order to prevent that, have guests bring their favorite holiday poems to read to the group during the holiday party, preferably after everyone has enjoyed a few drinks.

- **"Advent" by Rainer Maria Rilke**
- **"'Twas the Night Before Christmas" by Clement Clarke Moore**
- **"Der Stern" by Wilhelm Busch**
- **"The Oxen" by Thomas Hardy**

"Christmas is Christmas is Christmas is Christmas."
—Stanley Hudson

"Judgment is nigh, for the Belsnickel ist I!"

—Dwight Schrute

Yankee Swap

Whether you call it Yankee Swap, Nasty Christmas, or White Elephant, gift exchange games can be a fun and easy way to keep a holiday party interesting. As long as everyone is willing to follow the rules and play nice.

Set a price limit ahead of time to keep the swap fair. Each participant must bring a wrapped gift to the party.

Write out numbers on slips of paper that match the number of people who will be playing the game. Place the numbers in a hat or cup, and have each participant draw a number.

The person who picked number 1 begins the game and must select a package to unwrap.

The person who picked number 2 may choose a new gift to unwrap or steal the gift unwrapped by person 1. If a gift is stolen, the person who lost the gift may select a new gift or steal (if any gifts are available to steal). Repeat until all numbers have selected a gift.

Gifts may only be stolen two times. After a gift has been stolen twice, it is "locked" and will remain with the person who holds it.

After all participants have selected a gift, the person with number 1 can choose to trade their gift with any remaining unlocked gifts.

Group Holiday Photo

During the party, gather your coworkers for a group photo to share in your new Holiday Card Photo Frame (page 174). If you want things to seem more official, take the photo in front of the company sign. Otherwise, take the photo in front of your holiday decorations. Feel free to take a few, including serious and funny versions. But if for some reason you decide to take the photo outside, please make it quick. It's probably freezing out there!

TIP: Wear your Princess Unicorn Horns, Belsnickel attire, or Santa hats during the photo.

"Yankee Swap is like Machiavelli meets . . . Christmas."

—Dwight Schrute

DUNDER
MIFFLIN

"With two Santas in the room, things get ruthless."
—Michael Scott

DÉCOR

A well-decorated party sets the mood for the entire event. Decorate the office with sparkly garland, twinkle lights, and the biggest tree you can fit. The more decorations the better! You can also select from a list of possible holiday party themes—though a traditional Christmas is always an option!

Drape your food display with a festive red tablecloth, and provide red and green plates, napkins, and utensils. Set out Andy's Holiday Cheese Board (page 168), a Moroccan Christmas Mezze Platter (page 169), and Angela's Double-Fudge Brownies (page 170) to provide delicious bites for people to snack on throughout the party.

Set up a drink station with a big bowl of One-of-Anything Christmas Punch (page 171) along with any other alcoholic add-ins for partygoers to choose from.

Hang the crafted Holiday Garland (page 175) and Paper Snowflakes (page 172) on the walls and from the ceiling, and get ready to party.

"Most people don't even know that a candy cane represents a shepherd's crook, which I assure you does not taste like peppermint. It tastes like sheep feces."

—Dwight Schrute

POSSIBLE PARTY THEMES:

- Traditional Christmas
- Nutcracker Christmas
- Margarita-Karaoke Christmas
- Honolulu Christmas
- Moroccan Christmas
- Mo Rocca Christmas
- Classy Christmas
- Pennsylvania Dutch Christmas
- Tropical Christmas
- Topless Christmas
- Tapas Swiss Miss

Prank: Wrapping Paper Desk

There are few gifts that are better than laughter, and one surefire way to get almost everyone in the office chuckling is to individually gift wrap every single item on one of your coworker's desks. Okay, so one person might not be laughing as they spend hours removing the paper before they can get back to business as usual, but it's a small price to pay for the merriment of so many others. Want to really take things to the next level? Remove the actual desk entirely and wrap empty pieces of cardboard shaped like your coworker's desk to create a fake paper version for even more fun! You'll get bonus points if you create a fake wrapped chair as well. It's the gift that keeps on giving!

The Party's Over . . .

Well, there you have it. This is pretty much everything I ever learned watching the Dunder Mifflin Party Planning Committee. Whether you view the info lovingly gathered in these pages as a source of inspiration or merely as a collection of cautionary tales, these ideas are now yours to use as you see fit at future gatherings. Whatever the case, when the time comes for you to take the reins, I hope you realize your coworkers deserve to be celebrated any chance you get.

The Scranton branch of Dunder Mifflin was a truly special place because at the end of the day, the office wasn't really about selling paper. It was about people. It was more than just a building. It was a second home, whether most of the employees wanted to admit it or not. They shared the best moments of their lives together—from birthdays to weddings— and so many more. Hopefully with some of these tips you too can bring your office this close together.

No one said that starting a Party Planning Committee would be easy. On the show they were underappreciated, underfunded, and got thrown every curveball Michael could imagine. But even when things seemed impossible, that moment when a party finally came together and the smiles washed over everyone's faces, it seemed suddenly worth it.

And, hey, even if you manage to mess everything up, it likely won't be anywhere near as bad as some of the parties on the show. So just try to relax, and have some fun, okay? After all, this is a party . . .

"Party's over. You quit on Christmas, Christmas quits on you."

—Dwight Schrute

Notes:

Notes:

"The only time I set the bar low for is limbo."

—Michael Scott

INSIGHT EDITIONS

PO Box 3088
San Rafael, CA 94912
www.insighteditions.com

f Find us on Facebook: www.facebook.com/InsightEditions
🐦 Follow us on Twitter: @insighteditions

Library of Congress Cataloging-in-Publication Data available.

ISBN: 978-1-68383-943-9

Publisher: Raoul Goff
Associate Publisher: Vanessa Lopez
Creative Director: Chrissy Kwasnik
VP of Manufacturing: Alix Nicholaeff
Designer: Judy Wiatrek Trum
Senior Editor: Amanda Ng
Associate Editor: Maya Alpert
Editorial Assistant: Anna Wostenberg
Managing Editor: Lauren LePera
Production Editor: Jennifer Bentham
Production Director/Subsidiary Rights: Lina s Palma
Production Manager: Eden Orlesky

ROOTS of PEACE   REPLANTED PAPER

Insight Editions, in association with Roots of Peace, will plant two trees for each tree used in the manufacturing of this book. Roots of Peace is an internationally renowned humanitarian organization dedicated to eradicating land mines worldwide and converting war-torn lands into productive farms and wildlife habitats. Roots of Peace will plant two million fruit and nut trees in Afghanistan and provide farmers there with the skills and support necessary for sustainable land use.

Manufactured in China by Insight Editions

10 9 8 7 6 5 4 3 2 1

> "Hate to see you leave but love to watch you go. 'Cause of your butt."
>
> —Michael Scott